GEOGRAPHY TOO

Chapter and Section Support

LETTER HOME

The World of Geography

Social Studies Hot Line

Dear Family,

For the next few weeks, our social studies class will be studying geography. We will take a close look at the Earth and the people who live on it. In Chapter 1, we will study the five themes of geography: location, place, human-environment interaction, movement, and regions. Some of our topics will include climates and physical formations, human populations and cultures, and natural resources. If you have specific experience with or information about geography, please share it with your child.

We will be studying how geographers find exact locations and how physical features differ from place to place. We will learn about different types of maps. Looking at a map or a globe with your child can be a good way to discuss the material in this chapter. We are also learning to read map keys, to identify the scale of a map, and to understand how maps on flat surfaces can inaccurately represent shapes and distances. As you walk or drive in your neighborhood, you might notice significant landmarks that would be marked on a local map. Ask your child to make a local map or a list of places of interest around where you live.

If you read a newspaper with your child, you can discuss weather patterns and the climate in your area, an important part of your local geography. You might point out stories about different aspects of geography around the world, such as major landmarks or how people are moving from one country to another. You might also point out how we, as humans, are affecting our environment.

Look for more news about our class study of geography. I hope you and your child will enjoy sharing the study of geography with each other.

Sincerely,

CHAPTER 1
The World of Geography

The Five Themes of Geography

Lesson Objectives

Upon completion of this lesson, students will be able to
- define the scope of geography,
- identify the five themes of geography and relate each theme to real-world examples,
- use the five themes as a way to organize information about places.

Engage Motivate Students to Learn

Warm-Up Activity Have students write about what they think the subject of geography covers. Let them share their thoughts in a discussion. Ask students to create a preliminary definition of geography. Suggest that they record their definition and check it once or twice as they read the chapter. Encourage them to revise or rewrite their definition as they learn more about geography.

Activating Prior Knowledge Have students read Reach Into Your Background in the Before You Read box. Ask volunteers to describe how to get from their home to school. Use the directions as a springboard for listing other occasions in which they use geography in daily life.

Explore Develop Main Ideas

After students read the section, discuss the following aspects of geography: Why is the study of people and their activities part of geography? What is the difference between a natural and a cultural feature of a place? Give some examples. What are the two main questions that geographers ask? Why, for example, is a city in a particular place? What are some reasons people move from one place to another?

Teach Solicit Student Participation

Ask students to list the five themes of geography and then use them to create a chart with the following headings: *Theme, Definition,* and *Example.* Tell students that they can use examples from the text, but that original examples are preferred. The charts can be used in a discussion of how these themes will help them organize their thinking about a place. With the class, create a definition of geography that includes the five themes. This activity should take about 25 minutes.

Assess Assess Evidence of Learning

See the answers to the Section Review questions. Students may also demonstrate evidence of learning by completing the Guided Reading and Review and the Section Quiz from the *Teaching Resources.* If students are doing a book project, this may also demonstrate evidence of learning by showing progress on project preparation.

GUIDED READING AND REVIEW

The Five Themes of Geography

A. As You Read

Directions: As you read Section 1, answer the following questions in the space provided.

1. What two questions do geographers try to answer while studying different places?

   _____

2. How do the five themes—location, place, human-environment interaction, movement, and regions—help geographers when they study the Earth?

   _____

3. What are two different ways to describe a location?

   _____

4. Which way of describing location is being used when a geographer explains that a river is 250 miles north of San Antonio?

   _____

5. Why is the study of movement useful to geographers?

   _____

B. Reviewing Key Terms

Directions: Complete each sentence by writing the correct term in the blank provided.

6. The study of the Earth and its people is called _____ .

7. An invisible line that forms an east–west circle around the Earth is called both a(n)

   _____ and line of _____ .

8. An imaginary line that circles the Earth from north to south is called both a(n)

   _____ and line of _____ .

9. Geographers measure locations east or west of the _____ , which is numbered 0 degrees.

10. The parallel in the middle of the globe is called the _____ .

11. A unit used by geographers to measure location on maps is called a(n)

    _____ .

CHAPTER 1
The World
of Geography

The Five Themes of Geography

A. Key Terms and Concepts

Directions: Read the statements below. If a statement is true, write T in the blank provided. If it is false, write F. Rewrite false statements on another sheet of paper to make them true.

_____ **1.** The Prime Meridian runs through Greenwich, England.

_____ **2.** Lines of longitude circle the Earth parallel to the Equator.

_____ **3.** The Equator is an imaginary line that circles the globe at its widest point.

_____ **4.** The study of the Earth is called geography.

_____ **5.** Lines of latitude divide the globe into units called poles.

B. Main Ideas

Directions: Write the letter of the correct answer in each blank.

_____ **6.** Geographers study many things, including oceans, plant life, landforms, and
    a. geometry.
    b. comets.
    c. people.
    d. asteroids.

_____ **7.** Geographers use the five themes of geography to
    a. study world history.
    b. organize information.
    c. study world music.
    d. measure locations.

_____ **8.** To pinpoint the absolute location of a place, geographers use
    a. nearby landmarks.
    b. the Atlantic and Pacific oceans.
    c. the North and South poles.
    d. latitude and longitude.

_____ **9.** What does the theme of movement help geographers to understand?
    a. a location's physical and human features
    b. how people, goods, and ideas get from one place to another
    c. how far a place is from the Equator
    d. the climate of a place

_____ **10.** How do geographers use the theme of regions?
    a. to make comparisons
    b. to identify trade routes
    c. to locate places
    d. to show how people affect their environment

The Geographer's Tools

Lesson Objectives

Upon completion of this lesson, students will be able to
- analyze the problem of accurately representing a globe on a flat map,
- evaluate the advantages and disadvantages of various kinds of map projections,
- interpret the information provided on maps.

Engage Motivate Students to Learn

Warm-Up Activity Prepare the following demonstration for the class. Draw two same-size circles on an orange, one near the "Equator" of the orange, another near one of the "poles." Ask students what they think will happen to the circles if the orange is peeled and the peel is laid flat. Peel the orange and flatten the peel. Point out that the circles no longer appear the same size.

Activating Prior Knowledge Have students read Reach Into Your Background in the Before You Read box. Lead a discussion in which students list the kinds of maps they are familiar with. Prompt the discussion by asking how they find a particular store in a mall or how they find the fiction books in a library.

Explore Develop Main Ideas

Have students read the section. Then review with students the illustrations showing the variety of map projections. Help students use clues in the illustrations to answer the questions in each caption. Record their answers on the chalkboard.

Teach Solicit Student Participation

Ask students to work in small groups to develop a chart listing advantages and disadvantages of each type of projection. Challenge students to find at least three disadvantages—involving distance, shape, or size—in each map. Discuss why the Robinson map is the least distorted. This activity should take about 20 minutes.

Assess Assess Evidence of Learning

See the answers to the Section Review questions. Students may also demonstrate evidence of learning by completing the Guided Reading and Review and the Section Quiz from the *Teaching Resources*. If students are doing a book project, this may also demonstrate evidence of learning by showing progress on project preparation.

CHAPTER 1
The World
of Geography

The Geographer's Tools

2

A. As You Read

Directions: As you read Section 2, fill in the table below. Under each main idea, write two supporting statements.

Main Idea A
A long time ago, few people knew anything about the land and water beyond their homes or neighborhoods.

1. _____

_____

2. _____

_____

Main Idea B
Globes are an accurate way of presenting information about the Earth, but flat maps are generally a better way of mapping the Earth.

3. _____

_____

4. _____

_____

B. Reviewing Key Terms

Directions: Complete each sentence by writing the correct term in the blank provided.

5. When a landmass looks larger on a map than it does on the globe, that change in shape

   is called _____ .

6. The symbols that appear on a map are explained in the _____ , or legend.

7. A round ball called a(n) _____ shows the Earth in a smaller size,

   or _____ .

8. Geographers call a Mercator _____ a conformal map.

9. A map usually has a compass _____ showing the _____ , which are north, south, east, and west.

Name _____ Class _____ Date _____

The Geographer's Tools

A. Key Terms and Concepts

Directions: Fill in the blanks in Column I with the terms in Column II. Write the correct letter in each blank.

Column I

_____ **1.** A representation of the Earth on a flat piece of paper is called a ____ .

_____ **2.** A round model of the Earth is called a ____ .

_____ **3.** One of four compass points—north, east, south, and west—is called a ____ .

_____ **4.** All flat maps show some ____ , or misrepresentation, of the original shapes.

_____ **5.** A globe shows the Earth's continents on a much smaller ____ .

Column II

a. scale

b. cardinal direction

c. distortion

d. projection

e. globe

B. Main Ideas

Directions: Write the letter of the correct answer in each blank.

_____ **6.** People invented flat maps because globes cannot show
   a. names of continents.
   b. shapes of continents.
   c. enough detail.
   d. distance between contintents.

_____ **7.** What is a disadvantage of a Mercator projection?
   a. It does not include all the continents.
   b. It does not show many details of the Earth's surface.
   c. It is too large to be carried easily.
   d. It shows correct shapes but not true sizes.

_____ **8.** Why do many geographers prefer the Robinson projection?
   a. It accurately shows the size and shape of most of the land.
   b. It has no distortion of the Earth's surface.
   c. It is an interrupted projection of the Earth's surface.
   d. It is an equal-area map.

_____ **9.** To find the cardinal directions on a map, you should refer to the
   a. key.
   b. scale.
   c. compass rose.
   d. grid.

_____ **10.** To find the symbol used to show a road on a map, you should refer to the
   a. key.
   b. scale.
   c. compass rose.
   d. grid.

The World of Geography

Guiding Question:

- What is the Earth's geography like?

Geography is the study of the Earth. In their work, geographers are guided by two basic questions: (1) Where are things located? and (2) Why are they there? To find the answers, geographers use five themes to organize information. These themes are location (where a particular place exists), place (a location's physical and human features), human-environment inter-action (how people affect their environment), movement (how people, goods, and ideas get from one place to another), and regions (large areas that are linked by similar characteristics).

Geographers use special tools to study the Earth's surface. These include globes and different types of maps. Globes provide the most accurate rep-resentation of the Earth. Unfortunately, they are not easy to carry around and are too small to show much detail. Flat maps are easy to carry and can be very detailed, but maps present problems of their own. It is not possible to accurately show the round Earth on a flat surface without some distor-tion, or misrepresentation, of shapes and sizes. The Mercator projection is a flat map that sailors have used for over 400 years. It shows correct shapes of landmasses but not true distances or sizes. Today, many geographers prefer the Robinson projection, which shows sizes, shapes, and distances fairly accurately, but is distorted around the edges of the map.

Most maps have special parts, such as a compass rose, scale, key, and grid. A compass rose shows the cardinal directions: north, south, east, and west. The map scale tells you how much distance on land is represent-ed by a certain distance on the map. For example, on some maps an inch may equal one mile. On other maps, an inch may equal 100 miles. The key, or legend, explains the symbols for features such as roads and cities. A map grid helps people find things on the map. Some maps use a grid of parallels and meridians. Others have a grid of letters and numbers.

Name _____ Class _____ Date _____

CHAPTER
1

The World of Geography

Directions: Below is a list of key terms from Chapter 1. Write one sentence or phrase
on a separate sheet of paper that describes the meaning of each term. If necessary,
look in Chapter 1 to see how the terms are used.

1. **cardinal direction**—one of four compass points: north, south, east, and west

2. **compass rose**—a map feature that usually shows the four cardinal directions

3. **degree**—a unit of measure used to determine absolute location

4. **distortion**—in maps, a misrepresentation of the original shape

5. **Equator**—an imaginary line that circles the globe at its widest point

6. **geography**—the study of the Earth's surface, the connections between places, and the
relationships between people and their environment

7. **globe**—a round model of the Earth

8. **key**—the section of a map that explains the map symbols

9. **latitude lines**—a series of imaginary lines that circle the Earth parallel to the Equator;
also called parallels

10. **longitude lines**—a series of imaginary lines that run north and south from one pole
to the other; also called meridians

11. **meridian**—a line that circles the globe from north to south and runs through both the
North and the South poles

12. **parallel**—any of the imaginary lines that circle the Earth parallel to the Equator; a
latitude line

13. **plain**—a large area of flat or gently rolling land

14. **Prime Meridian**—the meridian, or longitude line, that runs through Greenwich,
England

15. **projection**—a representation of the Earth's rounded surface on a flat piece of paper

16. **scale**—the size or proportion of something on a map as compared to its actual size

The World of Geography

Directions: Use the information in Chapter 1 of your textbook to match each geographic theme in the box with an example. Write the letter of the matching theme on the line before the example. Then write two more sentences that give examples of the theme.

a. location	**d.** movement
b. place	**e.** regions
c. human-environment interaction	

_____ **1.** The Great Plains is one of the major wheat-growing areas in the world.

_____

_____

_____ **2.** Many New Englanders made their living by fishing until the stock of some species of fish in the coastal waters became depleted.

_____

_____

_____ **3.** St. Louis lies on the western bank of the Mississippi River in east central Missouri.

_____

_____

_____ **4.** Because it lies near both the ocean and the mountains, Vancouver, British Columbia, has a mild climate with rainy winters.

_____

_____

_____ **5.** Farmers from Germany settled in hilly areas of Missouri near rivers because these areas reminded them of their homeland.

_____

_____

ENRICHMENT

CHAPTER 1

The World of Geography

Maps Old and New

Directions: The two world maps below show how our knowledge of the geography of the world has changed over the past 500 years. The map on the top was done around 1490. The bottom map was created during the 1990s. Study and compare the maps. On another sheet of paper, complete the activities.

1. Describe the similarities between the map of 1490 and the contemporary map.

2. Describe the differences between the map of 1490 and the contemporary map.

3. Which area of the world did the mapmaker of 1490 seem to know the best?

4. How well do you know the world? From memory, draw an outline map of the world. Label as many continents, oceans, countries, seas, rivers, and lakes as you can. Then compare your map with a political map of the world.

The World of Geography

CHAPTER
1

Drawing Conclusions

Vegetation and Land Use Maps

Directions: A vegetation map shows the plant life that is native to an area. A land use map shows how an area of land is currently being used. Study these vegetation and land use maps of the United States. On another sheet of paper, answer the questions.

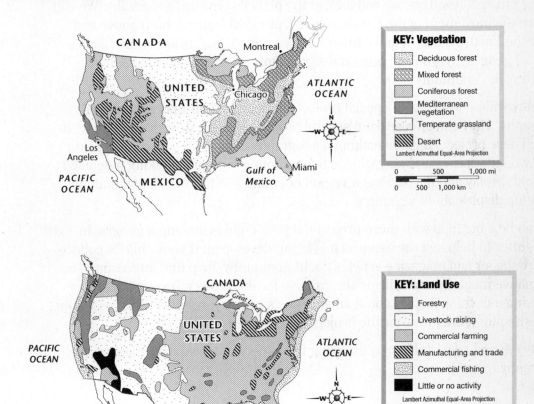

1. What are the two general types of native vegetation in the United States?

2. How is most of the land in the United States used?

3. How are most of the original grasslands in the United States being used?

4. What happened to most of the forests in the United States?

5. What conclusion can you draw about the effect that human beings have had on the native vegetation of the United States?

Name _____ Class _____ Date _____

Earth's Physical Geography

Social Studies Hot Line

Dear Family,

Our social studies class is continuing to explore the geography of the Earth. During the next few days, we will look at the planet's physical geography. We will explore the movement of the Earth in space, physical features both above and below the Earth's surface, and climates. As your child learns about the Earth's physical geography, you can point out significant geographic elements in or around your community.

Students will be working on special projects to deepen their understanding of geography. They can choose from several projects that are described in the textbook. These projects include making a geography card game, creating a poster display of newspaper and magazine articles about geography, making a detailed map and display about a particular region or country in the world, and making a desktop display about a country.

You can be a big help with these projects. If your child is making a geography card game, offer to help test the game as it is being developed. If your child is collecting newspaper and magazine articles about geography, help find interesting and informative magazines that he or she can use for the project. If your child is making a desktop display about an ancestor's country, suggest relatives whom he or she might interview for the project.

I hope you and your child enjoy studying the variety of topics that make up the geography of our planet.

Sincerely,

CHAPTER 2
Earth's Physical Geography

Our Planet, the Earth

Lesson Objectives

Upon completion of this lesson, students will be able to
- diagram how the Earth moves in space and its relation to the sun,
- describe how day and night are related to the rotation of the Earth,
- analyze the connection between the Earth's tilt and orbit around the sun and seasonal changes on the Earth.

Engage Motivate Students to Learn

Warm-Up Activity Ask students to orient themselves so that they can point to the east, where the sun rises, and the west, where the sun sets. (You may wish to have a directional compass on hand to confirm students' observations.)

Activating Prior Knowledge Have students read Reach Into Your Background in the Before You Read box. Ask students whether the type of clothes they wear, the activities they engage in, or the foods they eat change from season to season.

Explore Develop Main Ideas

After students read the section, have them describe the Earth's position in the solar system. Encourage them to include answers to the following questions in their descriptions. Why does a model of the solar system include moving planets? If the speed of the Earth's rotation were slower, how would it affect the cycle of day and night? How would a different slant to the axis of the Earth change the temperature of the surface of the Earth?

Teach Solicit Student Participation

Have students make a model of the Earth with clay, a round balloon, or a ball. Have them indicate the locations of the poles, the Equator, and the Southern and Northern hemispheres. Then have students use their models to demonstrate the Earth's rotation and revolution. This activity should take about 20 minutes.

Assess Assess Evidence of Learning

See the answers to the Section Review questions. Students may also demonstrate evidence of learning by completing the Guided Reading and Review and the Section Quiz from the *Teaching Resources*. If students are doing a book project, this may also demonstrate evidence of learning by showing progress on project preparation.

Name _____ Class _____ Date _____

Our Planet, the Earth

A. As You Read

Directions: As you read Section 1, answer the following questions in the space provided.

1. Why is our galaxy called the Milky Way?

   _____

   _____

2. Why are days longer than nights at certain times of the year?

   _____

   _____

3. When does the summer solstice occur in the Northern Hemisphere?

   _____

   _____

4. Why is it almost always hot in the area called the tropics?

   _____

   _____

B. Reviewing Key Terms

Directions: Complete each sentence by writing the correct term in the blank provided.

5. The imaginary line running through the Earth between the North and the South poles

   is called the _____ .

6. The polar zones are also called the _____ latitudes.

7. Temperate zones, or _____ latitudes, have different seasons throughout
   the year.

8. The oval-shaped path that the Earth takes around the sun is called a(n)

   _____ .

9. As the Earth travels around the sun, it spins on its axis, making a full

   _____ about every 24 hours.

10. Each year, the Earth makes one _____ around the sun.

11. It is almost always hot in the tropics, or _____ latitudes.

Earth's Physical Geography

CHAPTER 2
Earth's Physical
Geography

Our Planet, the Earth

A. Key Terms and Concepts

Directions: Match the definitions in Column I with the terms in Column II. Write the correct letter in each blank.

Column I

_____ 1. the regions between the Tropic of Cancer and the Arctic Circle, and the Tropic of Capricorn and the Antarctic Circle

_____ 2. a full orbit of the Earth around the sun

_____ 3. the spinning motion of the Earth

_____ 4. the path followed by the Earth as it travels around the sun

_____ 5. the region between the Tropic of Cancer and the Tropic of Capricorn

Column II

a. rotation

b. low latitudes

c. orbit

d. revolution

e. middle latitudes

B. Main Ideas

Directions: Write the letter of the correct answer in each blank.

_____ 6. As the Earth spins in space, on the side facing the sun it is always
  a. nighttime.
  b. daytime.
  c. winter.
  d. summer.

_____ 7. What factors cause changes in temperatures during the seasons?
  a. the high and middle latitudes
  b. the Earth's orbit and the Equator
  c. the Earth's tilt and orbit
  d. the Earth's longitude and the Tropic of Cancer

_____ 8. The climate in the polar zones is very cold because they receive
  a. only direct sunlight.
  b. both direct and indirect sunlight.
  c. no direct sunlight.
  d. no sunlight at all.

_____ 9. What is the result of the sun being directly over the Equator on March 21 and September 23?
  a. Days and nights are unequal in length.
  b. It is daytime for almost 20 hours.
  c. It is nighttime for almost 20 hours.
  d. Days are almost exactly as long as nights.

_____ 10. The sun shines directly over the Tropic of Cancer in the Northern Hemisphere on the
  a. summer solstice.
  b. winter solstice.
  c. spring equinox.
  d. fall equinox.

Land, Air, and Water

Lesson Objectives

Upon completion of this lesson, students will be able to
- identify the materials the Earth is made of and the landforms it contains;
- describe forces that shape the land, such as volcanoes, earthquakes, weathering, and erosion;
- investigate the theory of plate tectonics;
- analyze the role water plays in the Earth's geography.

Engage Motivate Students to Learn

Warm-Up Activity Have students sort photos of landscapes by the different landforms, such as mountains, hills, seashores, plains, and plateaus, and make a poster collage. As they complete the chapter, they can return to their posters and label the landforms represented.

Activating Prior Knowledge Have students read Reach Into Your Background in the Before You Read box. Encourage students to describe how activities such as skiing or biking change as land changes from flat to hilly.

Explore Develop Main Ideas

After students read the section, have them discuss the following questions. What do geographers who study volcanoes and earthquakes learn about the Earth? Why is it important to study what's happening under the ocean? What leads scientists to think that South America and Africa once fit together like puzzle pieces? How are the massive plates of the Earth's surface able to move?

Teach Solicit Student Participation

Have students trace the continents to make a puzzle map of the world. Have them use the maps in the section as references and experiment with moving the continents in the directions indicated. This activity should take about 30 minutes.

Assess Assess Evidence of Learning

See the answers to the Section Review questions. Students may also demonstrate evidence of learning by completing the Guided Reading and Review and the Section Quiz from the *Teaching Resources.* If students are doing a book project, it may also demonstrate evidence of learning by showing progress on project preparation.

Land, Air, and Water

A. As You Read

Directions: As you read Section 2, fill in the table below with information about continents. Under each main idea, write two supporting statements.

Main Idea A
Geographers theorize that millions of years ago, there was only one giant landmass, called Pangaea, on the Earth.
1. _____   _____
2. _____   _____
Main Idea B
The continents are parts of plates in the Earth's crust that over time move and shift in different directions.
3. _____   _____
4. _____   _____

B. Reviewing Key Terms

Directions: Complete each sentence by writing the correct term in the blank provided.

5. A landform that is wide at the bottom and rises more than 2,000 feet (610 m) above sea level to a narrow peak is called a(n) _____ . A landform that is lower with a rounded top is called a(n) _____ .

6. A flat area or an area with gently rolling land is called a(n) _____ .

7. A flat area that rises above the surrounding land is called a(n) _____ .

8. A shape or type of land, such as a mountain or hill, is called a(n) _____ .

9. Each huge piece of the Earth's crust is called a(n) _____ .

10. The idea that the Earth's outer skin is broken into huge plates is the theory of _____ .

SECTION QUIZ

Land, Air, and Water

A. Key Terms and Concepts

Directions: Read each statement below. If a statement is true, write T in the blank provided. If it is false, write F. On another sheet of paper, rewrite false statements to make them true.

_____ **1.** Large areas of flat or gently rolling land are called plains.

_____ **2.** According to the theory of plate tectonics, the Earth's crust is made up of one unbroken piece, or plate.

_____ **3.** The breaking down of rocks by construction equipment is called weathering.

_____ **4.** The band of gases that surrounds the Earth is called the atmosphere.

_____ **5.** Mountains and hills are examples of landforms.

B. Main Ideas

Directions: Write the letter of the correct answer in each blank.

_____ **6.** What is a landform that usually rises more than 2,000 feet (610 m) above sea level?
    a. a plateau   **c.** a mountain
    b. a hill   **d.** a valley

_____ **7.** Two hundred million years ago, all the land on Earth was
    a. underwater.   **c.** covered with forests.
    b. part of one huge landmass.   **d.** part of the Ring of Fire.

_____ **8.** What are three things that cause weathering?
    a. wind, rain, and ice   **c.** erosion, magma, and extreme heat
    b. earthquakes, volcanoes, and rain   **d.** tidal waves, earthquakes, and extreme cold

_____ **9.** The atmosphere surrounding the Earth provides life-giving oxygen for
    a. rocks.   **c.** people and animals.
    b. plants.   **d.** fish in the ocean.

_____ **10.** Weathering and erosion break down rocks and slowly create
    a. oxygen to plants.   **c.** tectonic plates.
    b. the Earth's poles.   **d.** new landforms.

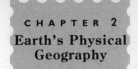

CHAPTER 2
Earth's Physical
Geography

Climate and What Influences It

Chapter and Section Support

Lesson Objectives

Upon completion of this lesson, students will be able to
- describe the differences between weather and climate,
- identify the ways in which landforms and bodies of water affect weather and climate,
- trace wind and water currents and describe their effects on climate and weather.

Engage Motivate Students to Learn

Warm-Up Activity Ask students to think of as many words as they can to describe weather conditions, and make a list of their suggestions. Encourage them to use the dictionary and thesaurus to increase their list. Then ask them to choose the words that best describe the weather today, and those that describe the different seasons where they live. Students can return to the list as they complete the chapter, adding new words or using those they thought of to describe the climates they investigate.

Activating Prior Knowledge Have students read Reach Into Your Background in the Before You Read box. Some students may not have experienced severe storms. Invite them to talk about storms they've heard about or seen on films. Ask how they think they would feel and what they would do to stay safe.

Explore Develop Main Ideas

Once students have read the section, ask them to discuss the following questions. Why does the sun rise earlier during the summer months than during the winter months? What makes some months colder than others? What is the deciding factor between rain and snow?

Teach Solicit Student Participation

Have students keep a weather record on daily weather conditions such as temperature, precipitation, and wind direction. Have them record observations each day for one week. Use these weather records as the basis for a discussion about weather and climate in your region. This activity should take 10 minutes each day, and 15 minutes for discussion at the end of the week.

Assess Assess Evidence of Learning

See the answers to the Section Review questions. Students may also demonstrate evidence of learning by completing the Guided Reading and Review and the Section Quiz from the *Teaching Resources.* If students are doing a book project, this may also demonstrate evidence of learning by showing progress on project preparation.

GUIDED READING AND REVIEW

Climate and What Influences It

A. As You Read

Directions: As you read Section 3, complete the statements below.

1. The climate of an area is the average _____ over many years.

2. Fast moving rivers in the ocean, called _____ , are caused by the Earth's rotation.

3. In the summertime, a town near a lake or an ocean will usually be _____ than an area farther away from the water.

4. As well as making climates milder, wind and water can cause _____ to develop.

5. Violent wind and rain storms that form over the tropics in the Atlantic Ocean are called

   _____ . Similar storms that form over the Pacific Ocean are called

   _____ .

6. Tornadoes are twisting and swirling funnels of _____ that can sometimes reach 200 miles per hour.

B. Reviewing Key Terms

Directions: In the blanks provided, write the definitions for the following key terms.

7. weather

   _____

   _____

8. temperature

   _____

   _____

9. precipitation

   _____

   _____

10. climate

   _____

   _____

Name _____ Class _____ Date _____

CHAPTER 2
Earth's Physical
Geography

Climate and What Influences It

A. Key Terms and Concepts
Directions: Fill in the blanks in Column I with the terms in Column II. Write the correct letter in each blank.

Column I

_____ 1. In India, people have serious reasons for watching the _____ , or daily changes in the air.

_____ 2. The degree of hotness or coldness of any-thing, such as air or water, is called its _____ .

_____ 3. A current in the Atlantic Ocean that travels north and east from the tropics is _____ .

_____ 4. The water that falls to the ground as rain, sleet, hail, or snow is called _____ .

_____ 5. The current that moves north from Antarctica up the coast of South America is _____ .

Column II

a. temperature

b. precipitation

c. the Peruvian Current

d. weather

e. the Gulf Stream

B. Main Ideas
Directions: Write the letter of the correct answer in each blank.

_____ 6. The weather pattern of an area over a long period of time is its
   a. precipitation.
   b. weather.
   c. climate.
   d. temperature.

_____ 7. What would happen to the Earth without wind and water?
   a. It would become too cold.
   b. It would overheat.
   c. It wouldn't rotate evenly.
   d. It wouldn't orbit the sun.

_____ 8. Why is it always cooler by the water on a hot summer day?
   a. Water makes up most of the Earth's surface.
   b. Currents travel great distances.
   c. Water takes longer to heat or cool than land does.
   d. Warm water moves north.

_____ 9. Storms are important to people because they
   a. bring life-giving water.
   b. make climates milder.
   c. always cause tidal waves.
   d. help to cool the land.

_____ 10. Both winds and ocean currents are created by
   a. the Earth's rotation.
   b. the Earth's revolution.
   c. rising hot air.
   d. tall mountains.

© Prentice-Hall, Inc.

How Climate Affects Vegetation

Lesson Objectives

Upon completion of this lesson, students will be able to
- identify, compare, and contrast the major climate regions of the Earth,
- describe the kinds of vegetation found in different climate regions,
- analyze how temperature, precipitation, and elevation affect climate in a region.

Engage Motivate Students to Learn

Warm-Up Activity Ask students what they think would be different about their lives if they lived in a different climate region. Would the school building or their homes be constructed differently? Would they wear different clothes? Eat different foods? Play different games or sports? Ask them to describe what they think might be the advantages or disadvantages of living in a different climate.

Activating Prior Knowledge Have students read Reach Into Your Background in the Before You Read box. Ask them to name or describe the plants, bushes, and trees around them. How do they stay alive? How do they propagate? Do they show signs of seasonal change?

Explore Develop Main Ideas

Direct students to read the section. Suggest that, as they read, they keep in mind the following questions. Why can some plants survive better in one climate than in another? Are there plants that can survive in all climates? Why do climates change? Why is the study of fossils useful when investigating climate and change? What might happen to a climate region after a change in the landforms of the region, such as might happen in an earthquake or a volcanic eruption?

Teach Solicit Student Participation

Have students create a chart with a column for each of the climate regions discussed in the text: *tropical climate; dry climate; moderate climate; humid continental climate; subarctic continental climate,* and *polar climate.* Have them fill in the chart with facts they draw from the section. Suggest that they include information from the rainfall and temperature maps. Use the completed chart as a resource for a discussion of the similarities and differences in different regions. This activity should take about 30 minutes.

Assess Assess Evidence of Learning

See the answers to the Section Review questions. Students may also demonstrate evidence of learning by completing the Guided Reading and Review and the Section Quiz from the *Teaching Resources.* If students are doing a book project, this may also demonstrate evidence of learning by showing progress on project preparation.

CHAPTER 2
Earth's Physical Geography

How Climate Affects Vegetation

A. As You Read

Directions: As you read Section 4, fill in the table below with details about tropical, moderate, and polar climates.

Vegetation and Climate

	Tropical Climate	Moderate Climate	Polar Climate
Location	1.	2.	3.
Vegetation	4.	5.	6.
Seasons	7.	8.	9.

B. Reviewing Key Terms

Directions: In the blanks provided, write the definitions for the following key terms.

10. vegetation

_____

_____

11. canopy

_____

_____

12. tundra

_____

_____

13. vertical climate

_____

_____

Name _____ Class _____ Date _____

How Climate Affects Vegetation

A. Key Terms and Concepts

Directions: Match the definitions in Column I with the terms in Column II. Write the correct letter in each blank.

Column I

_____ **1.** a layer of branches and leaves at the tops of the trees in a forest

_____ **2.** a cold region where only certain plants, such as low grasses, can grow

_____ **3.** the overall weather patterns of an area as influenced by elevation

_____ **4.** the plants in an area

_____ **5.** area in the United States with very tall grass

Column II

a. tundra

b. vegetation

c. Great Plains

d. vertical climate

e. canopy

B. Main Ideas

Directions: Write the letter of the correct answer in each blank.

_____ **6.** What do plants need to survive in a particular climate?
    a. roots, water, and wind
    b. vines, food, and rain
    c. water, sunlight, and certain nutrients
    d. vegetation, adaptations, and sunlight

_____ **7.** Geographers discuss five broad types of climates: tropical, dry, moderate, continental, and
    a. rain forest.
    b. polar.
    c. desert.
    d. ocean.

_____ **8.** Because arid and semiarid climates receive little rain, plants grow
    a. very deep roots.
    b. far apart in sandy soil.
    c. large, fleshy leaves.
    d. close together in rich soil.

_____ **9.** Since temperatures in moderate climates hardly ever fall below freezing, the vegetation in these areas is
    a. limited to grass only.
    b. limited to trees only.
    c. limited to shrubs only.
    d. widely varied.

_____ **10.** Why is there no vegetation at the top of Mount Everest?
    a. It is too cold to support any plant life.
    b. There's no oxygen or carbon dioxide there.
    c. It is too wet for plants to survive.
    d. The sunlight is too strong for plants.

Earth's Physical Geography

Guiding Question:

- What is the Earth's geography like?

The physical geography of the Earth includes its land, air, water, climate, and vegetation. The movement of the planet through space affects all of these features. The Earth rotates once a day on its tilted axis, causing day and night. As the Earth orbits the sun once a year, the tilt of its axis causes changes in the lengths of day and night, as well as changes in temperatures. These temperature changes cause the seasons.

Scientists think that 200 million years ago, all the land on the Earth was part of a single supercontinent, known as Pangaea. Over millions of years, Pangaea broke apart, forming the separate continents we know today. Scientists use a theory called plate tectonics to explain why Pangaea broke apart. Huge masses of land, or tectonic plates, slowly float on magma below them, altering the shape of the Earth's surface. When the plates rub against one another, the movement can cause earthquakes and volcanoes.

Weathering and erosion are two forces that slowly break down landforms on the Earth's surface. After the landforms have been broken down, erosion carries the material to different places, where new landforms are created. Wind, rain, and ice all play a part in these processes.

The Earth is surrounded by a thick layer of special gases called the atmosphere. The atmosphere keeps the planet warm and provides oxygen and carbon dioxide for animals and plants.

Weather is the day-to-day changes in air temperature and precipitation. Climate is the average weather over many years for a particular region. Climate is affected by latitude and by the movement of winds and ocean currents. Geographers have identified five broad types of climates: tropical, dry, moderate, continental, and polar. Each has its unique vegetation, temperature, rainfall, and seasons.

VOCABULARY ACTIVITY

Earth's Physical Geography

Directions: Match the definitions in Column I with the key terms in Column II. Write the correct letter in each blank. If necessary, look up the terms in your textbook glossary.

Column I

_____ 1. one complete orbit of the Earth around the sun

_____ 2. the spinning motion of the Earth

_____ 3. a landform with a rounded top that is lower and less steep than a mountain

_____ 4. the Earth's path around the sun

_____ 5. the plants in an area

_____ 6. the region between the Tropic of Cancer and the Tropic of Capricorn

_____ 7. a large, mostly flat area that rises above the surrounding land

_____ 8. the regions between the Arctic Circle and the North Pole, and the Antarctic Circle and the South Pole

_____ 9. in geography, a huge section of the Earth's crust

_____ 10. water that falls to the ground from the atmosphere

_____ 11. a landform that rises usually more than 2,000 feet above sea level

_____ 12. the band of gases that surrounds the Earth

_____ 13. a large area of flat or gently rolling land

_____ 14. the weather patterns that an area experiences over time

_____ 15. the degree of hotness or coldness of a substance

_____ 16. day-to-day changes in the air

Column II

a. atmosphere

b. climate

c. high latitudes

d. hill

e. low latitudes

f. mountain

g. orbit

h. plain

i. plate

j. plateau

k. precipitation

l. revolution

m. rotation

n. temperature

o. vegetation

p. weather

© Prentice-Hall, Inc.

Earth's Physical Geography

Directions: Use the information in Chapter 2 of your textbook to help you list at least one effect of each cause.

Earth's Physical Geography

Cause	Effect
The Earth rotates on its axis in an orbit around the sun.	1.
The Earth's axis is at an angle.	2.
Pangaea split into several pieces that moved apart.	3.
The plates that make up the Earth's crust move apart and magma leaks out.	4.
The Earth's plates push against each other.	5.
Weathering and erosion go on continually.	6.
A region lies in the middle latitudes.	7.
Hot air rises and circulates toward cooler regions, while cold air stays low and moves toward warmer regions.	8.
A city is located near an ocean.	9.

Name _____ Class _____ Date _____

Earth's Physical Geography

Tropics of Cancer and Capricorn

Directions: Read the passage and complete the activities.

Two lines of latitude form the boundaries of the region known as the tropics. These two lines are the Tropic of Cancer and the Tropic of Capricorn. They mark the farthest places north and south of the Equator where the sun ever shines directly overhead.

The Tropic of Cancer is 23°27′ north of the Equator. The sun shines directly overhead on the Tropic of Cancer at noon around June 21. That day is the summer solstice, the longest day of the year, in the Northern Hemisphere. The sun is then at its farthest distance north of the Equator. The sun appears in the constellation, or formation of stars, called Gemini at that time. But the Tropic of Cancer is named after the constellation Cancer because the sun appeared in that constellation in 2 B.C. That was when the constellations were named and when the Tropic of Cancer got its name.

The Tropic of Capricorn is 23°27′ south of the Equator. The sun shines directly overhead on the Tropic of Capricorn at noon around December 21. That day is the winter solstice, or shortest day of the year, in the Northern Hemisphere. The sun is then at its farthest distance south of the Equator. The sun appears in the constellation Sagittarius at that time. But it appeared in the constellation Capricorn at the time the Tropic of Capricorn was named.

Over time, the direction of the Earth's axis gradually changes. In about 24,000 years, the sun will again appear in the constellations of Cancer and Capricorn at the summer and winter solstices.

1. Explain the significance of the Tropic of Cancer and the Tropic of Capricorn.

2. What is unusual about the names *Tropic of Cancer* and *Tropic of Capricorn?*

3. What is a solstice?

4. Draw a map showing the locations of the Equator, the Tropic of Cancer, and the Tropic of Capricorn. Then draw diagrams showing the positions of the sun and the Earth during the summer and winter solstices in the Northern Hemisphere. Use reference books to find the information you need.

Name _____ Class _____ Date _____

Earth's Physical Geography

Distinguishing Fact From Opinion

Directions: The chart lists evidence supporting the theory that all of the Earth's continents were once part of a huge landmass called Pangaea. Based on the information in the chart, decide whether the statements that follow are fact or opinion. Write *F* or *O* before each statement.

Evidence Supporting Theory of Continental Drift

Evidence	Where Found
Fossils of reptile called lystrosaurus	Antarctica, China, India, Southern Africa
Fossils of opossums	North America, Siberia
Fossils of reptile called mesosaurus	Brazil, South Africa
Fossils of fern called glossopteris	Australia, India
Matching rocks	Mountains in South Africa and Argentina

_____ **1.** Similar fossils have been found on continents that today are widely separated by oceans.

_____ **2.** The fossil evidence absolutely proves that Pangaea existed.

_____ **3.** The theory of continental drift is far-fetched.

_____ **4.** Other theories might explain why fossils of the same animal or plant appear on widely separated continents.

_____ **5.** The existence of matching rocks on separate continents supports the theory of continental drift.

© Prentice-Hall, Inc.

LETTER HOME

Earth's Human Geography

Social Studies Hot Line

Dear Family,

In the next few days, our social studies class will explore the human geography of the Earth. We will learn where most of the people in the world live and why, how the population is growing, and why people migrate. If you have any personal or family stories about migration, they could provide an excellent means to discuss some of the information in this chapter.

As you drive or travel around your neighborhood or local area, notice with your child how densely populated it is. Talk about the factors that might influence population density. These could include climate, landforms, or access to rivers, lakes, or oceans. Encourage your child to estimate the population density where you live (the total number of people divided by the number of square miles or square kilometers).

Look for articles or news reports about population growth and the pressures that it is causing throughout the world. They can provide you with a good beginning to a discussion about the material in Chapter 3. Articles could include topics such as food shortages, overcrowded cities, unemployment, and human migrations. If you have access to the Internet, you and your child might search together to find information about population and immigration in different parts of the world.

You'll be receiving more information during the coming weeks about the cultures and natural resources of the world. Have fun as you share the wonderful world of geography with your child.

Sincerely,

CHAPTER 3
Earth's Human Geography

Where Do People Live?

Lesson Objectives

Upon completion of this lesson, students will be able to
- describe factors that cause large populations in some parts of the world and limit population in other parts;
- explain how population density is measured, and name a city, country, and continent with a dense population;
- summarize how the geography of a country helps determine the size of its population.

Engage Motivate Students to Learn

Warm-Up Activity Briefly tell students the story of Robinson Crusoe, who was shipwrecked on a desert island. Then have students make a geography "survival chart" telling what kind of climate would help them live comfortably on the island. Encourage them to think about what landforms and vegetation would be best. Direct students to list additional geographic features they think might make the island an easier place on which to live.

Activating Prior Knowledge Have students read Reach Into Your Background in the Before You Read box. Have students record their lists and then, as a class, indicate which things would make survival easier and which might make survival more difficult.

Explore Develop Main Ideas

Have students read the section, looking for answers to the following questions: What are some important characteristics about the places where people live? How do climate and landforms affect where people live? Why does the United States have a large population, while Canada has a small population?

Teach Solicit Student Participation

Have students create charts to organize facts from the section. Use their completed charts to discuss the factors that seem to affect population distribution. This activity should take about 20 minutes.

Assess Assess Evidence of Learning

See the answers to the Section Review questions. Students may also demonstrate evidence of learning by completing the Guided Reading and Review and the Section Quiz from the *Teaching Resources*. If students are doing a book project, this may also demonstrate evidence of learning by showing progress on project preparation.

Name _____ Class _____ Date _____

Where Do People Live?

A. As You Read

Directions: As you read Section 1, answer the following questions in the space provided.

1. What three things do demographers examine to understand population distribution?

_____

2. How much of the Earth is covered by oceans?

_____

3. What areas are difficult for people to live in?

_____

4. Along what types of geographic features did most major civilizations begin?

_____

5. Why did few people settle in the Great Plains of the United States at first?

_____

6. How do some people manage to live comfortably in extremely hot or cold climates?

_____

B. Reviewing Key Terms

Directions: In the blanks provided below, write the definitions for the following key terms.

7. population

_____

_____

8. population distribution

_____

_____

9. demographer

_____

_____

10. population density

_____

_____

SECTION QUIZ

CHAPTER 3
Earth's Human
Geography

Where Do People Live?

1

Chapter and Section Support

A. Key Terms and Concepts

Directions: Read the statements below. If a statement is true, write T in the blank provided. If it is false, write F. Rewrite false statements on another sheet of paper to make them true.

_____ **1.** A demographer studies the geography of the Earth.

_____ **2.** The way in which a population is spread out over an area is called population distribution.

_____ **3.** Population density is the total number of people living in a given area.

_____ **4.** The population of the world is the total number of people living on the Earth.

_____ **5.** The Nile River valley has one of the lowest population densities in the world.

B. Main Idea

Directions: Write the letter of the correct answer in each blank.

_____ **6.** In which of the following areas would you expect many people to live?
- **a.** mountainous area
- **b.** flat area near a river
- **c.** hot, dry desert
- **d.** Pacific Ocean

_____ **7.** Which of the following characteristics tells you that a continent might have a low population density?
- **a.** fertile soil
- **b.** rich natural resources
- **c.** few rivers and little rainfall
- **d.** good climates

_____ **8.** To find the population density of a place, divide the number of people living there by the number of
- **a.** mountains.
- **b.** rivers.
- **c.** square miles or kilometers.
- **d.** countries.

_____ **9.** On a world population map, level areas near bodies of water have
- **a.** a higher population density.
- **b.** a lower population distribution.
- **c.** an average population.
- **d.** a lower population density.

_____ **10.** To survive in harsh desert environments, people have developed
- **a.** pipelines to move water from other places.
- **b.** advanced technology to make water from sand.
- **c.** the ability to survive with no drinking water.
- **d.** ways of life suited to desert environments.

© Prentice-Hall, Inc.

A Growing Population

Lesson Objectives

Upon completion of this lesson, students will be able to
- describe two main reasons why the world's population is rapidly increasing,
- explain some of the problems that rapid population growth is causing.

Engage Motivate Students to Learn

Warm-Up Activity Point out to students that over the last hundred years or so, the average number of children per family in the United States has decreased. Have students suggest some reasons for the change in the size of families. Ask them to suggest some ways in which this change affects how people live.

Activating Prior Knowledge Have students read Reach Into Your Background in the Before You Read box. Have students choose representatives to call their city or town hall to find out the number of births and deaths that occurred in your community last year.

Explore Develop Main Ideas

As students read this section, have them think about these key questions: Why was population growth slower in past centuries? What factors have contributed to the world's recent rapid population growth? How does rapid population growth affect the environment today in many parts of the world?

Teach Solicit Student Participation

Have the class discuss the impact of rapid population growth on the environment. Ask students to name several factors that affect population growth and to write an explanation of how each factor works to increase or decrease population growth. Ask them to indicate which factor they feel is the most important and give reasons for their opinions.

Assess Assess Evidence of Learning

See the answers to the Section Review questions. Students may also demonstrate evidence of learning by completing the Guided Reading and Review and the Section Quiz from the *Teaching Resources*. If students are doing a book project, it may also demonstrate evidence of learning by showing progress on project preparation.

Name _____ Class _____ Date _____

GUIDED READING AND REVIEW

Name _____ Class _____ Date _____

CHAPTER 3
Earth's Human Geography

A Growing Population

A. As You Read

Directions: As you read Section 2, fill in the table below with information about population growth.

Causes and Effects of Population Growth

Cause	Effect
A hundred years ago in the United States, the death rate was higher, food supplies were scarce, and many died of diseases.	1.
The birthrate has increased quickly and the death rate has slowed.	2.
New medicines and types of surgery treat health problems and fight diseases.	3.
4.	Some nations in Southwest Asia face shortages of fresh water and energy.
5.	Forests in India and Pakistan are disappearing, affecting the supply of clean air.

B. Reviewing Key Terms

Directions: Complete each sentence by writing the correct term in the blank.

6. The average number of years a woman in the United States is projected to live, also known as her_____ , is 80 years.

7. The changes made in farming methods during the 1950s are called the_____ .

8. The number of live births per 1,000 people each year is called the_____ .

9. When a country's birthrate is higher than its _____ , its population is growing.

SECTION QUIZ

A Growing Population

A. Key Terms and Concepts

Directions: Match the definitions in Column I with the terms in Column II. Write the correct letter in each blank.

Column I

_____ **1.** the number of deaths each year per 1,000 people

_____ **2.** changes in agriculture since the 1950s that have greatly increased the world's food supply

_____ **3.** how long a person may be expected to live

_____ **4.** the number of live births each year per 1,000 people

_____ **5.** medicine used to fight a disease

Column II

a. Green Revolution

b. death rate

c. life expectancy

d. vaccine

e. birthrate

B. Main Ideas

Directions: Write the letter of the correct answer in each blank.

_____ **6.** In modern times, the world's population has
  a. decreased.   **c.** grown slowly.
  b. grown greatly.   **d.** not changed.

_____ **7.** Demographers are able to figure out population growth by comparing
  a. the life expectancies of men and women.   **c.** birthrates and death rates.
  b. diseases around the world.   **d.** food supplies around the world.

_____ **8.** How have scientific advancements in medicine and farming methods affected the world's population?
  a. People live longer than ever.   **c.** The death rate has increased.
  b. More babies are born with serious health problems.   **d.** The birthrate has decreased.

_____ **9.** Stable populations use resources, such as food and fresh water, much more slowly than populations that are
  a. in the United States.   **c.** shrinking.
  b. in Europe.   **d.** growing.

_____ **10.** Rapid population growth causes which bad effect on the environment?
  a. fewer jobs for more people   **c.** shrinking forests in India
  b. more trees to hold soil in place   **d.** clean waterways

CHAPTER 3
Earth's Human
Geography

Why People Migrate

Lesson Objectives

Upon completion of this lesson, students will be able to
- list several reasons why people migrate to new places,
- explain how the "push-pull" theory describes the process of immigration,
- analyze urbanization as a factor in the migration of people in many different lands.

Engage Motivate Students to Learn

Warm-Up Activity Ask students how many of them have lived in another city, state, or country. Then ask whether they remember what it was like when their families moved. What things did they find familiar? What things were new or different? Did they feel at home in the new place at first? Ask them to describe how they made friends at school and with neighbors.

Activating Prior Knowledge Have students read Reach Into Your Background in the Before You Read box. Invite students to discuss how they react when children from other cities, towns, or countries move into their neighborhood. Have them describe what they can do to make the newcomers feel welcome.

Explore Develop Main Ideas

The United States is often called "a nation of immigrants." As students read the section, ask what evidence they can find to support this statement. What peoples came here from other parts of the world in the 1800s? What peoples arrived in the United States during the 1900s? What were some reasons for their migration?

Teach Solicit Student Participation

Have students create a two-column chart, *The "Push-Pull" of Migration*. Have students fill in each column of their chart with facts from the section. When they have completed their charts, have them rank the items in each column by numbering them from most to least important. This activity should take about 20 minutes.

Assess Assess Evidence of Learning

See the answers to the Section Review questions. Students may also demonstrate evidence of learning by completing the Guided Reading and Review and the Section Quiz from the *Teaching Resources*. If students are doing a book project, this may also demonstrate evidence of learning by showing progress on project preparation.

Name _____ Class _____ Date _____

Why People Migrate

A. As You Read

Directions: As you read Section 3, fill in the table below with information about migration. Under each main idea, write two supporting statements.

Main Idea A
The "push-pull" theory explains many immigration trends in history.

1. _____

_____

2. _____

_____

Main Idea B
Although many people leave their own countries for others, migration can occur within a country, too.

3. _____

_____

4. _____

_____

B. Reviewing Key Terms

Directions: Complete each sentence by writing the correct term in the blank provided.

5. The idea that certain reasons, often economic, cause people to move from one place to another is known as the _____ .

6. A person who _____ , or moves from one place to another, is called a(n)

_____ .

7. A city or town is sometimes called a(n) _____ area. A less populated village is sometimes called a(n) _____ area.

8. Many people move from small towns to cities. This movement is called

_____ .

CHAPTER 3
Earth's Human
Geography

Why People Migrate

A. Key Terms and Concepts

Directions: Match the definitions in Column I with the terms in Column II. Write the correct letter in each blank.

Column I

_____ 1. a person who moves to a new country in order to settle there

_____ 2. an area with a low population density, such as the countryside

_____ 3. the movement of people from one country or region to another

_____ 4. the movement of people to cities

_____ 5. an area with a large population density, such as a city

Column II

a. migration

b. urban area

c. urbanization

d. rural area

e. immigrant

B. Main Ideas

Directions: Write the letter of the correct answer in each blank.

_____ 6. Which of the following is an economic reason why people migrate?
   a. They do not like the government.
   b. They cannot find work.
   c. They are fleeing a war.
   d. They are persecuted for their religion.

_____ 7. How do demographers use the "push-pull" theory?
   a. to explain climactic change
   b. to explain immigration
   c. to describe political change
   d. to describe geographic change

_____ 8. In the 1840s and 1850s, many people left Ireland for the United States because they
   a. were starving.
   b. were fleeing from war.
   c. wanted better jobs.
   d. wanted to live in large cities.

_____ 9. Recently, people in the United States have been moving to southern and southwestern states to find
   a. better transportation systems.
   b. better schools.
   c. better jobs or a better climate.
   d. freedom to practice their religion.

_____ 10. Because of rapid population growth, São Paulo, Brazil, cannot provide its citizens with enough
   a. houses and jobs.
   b. cars.
   c. television sets.
   d. radios.

CHAPTER SUMMARY

CHAPTER 3

Earth's Human Geography

Guiding Question:

• Where do the world's people live?

Most of the people in the world live in regions that are near major bodies of water, have fertile soil, and have a moderate climate with adequate rainfall. The most populated continents are Asia, Europe, and North America. People tend to live in places where they can trade, grow crops, and use natural resources. The other continents—South America, Africa, and Australia—have smaller populations because it is harder to live there. Although these continents have some areas that are excellent for living, they also contain harsh deserts, high mountains, and dense rain forests, which do not support large numbers of people.

During the 1900s, the birthrate has increased while the death rate has decreased. The result has been an incredibly rapid growth in population, caused by a larger food supply and advances in medicine. In some countries, the population doubles in under 20 years. People now live longer than ever. A hundred years ago, people in the United States usually lived less than 50 years. Today, the average life expectancy for women is about 80 years and for men about 73 years.

For centuries, people have moved from one place to another. This is called migration. Immigrants are people who leave one country and move to another. Demographers, scientists who study human populations, use the "push-pull" theory to explain immigration. It says people are pushed from their homelands by poor economic or political conditions. These people are pulled by the hope of a better life somewhere else. In many places, more and more people are moving from rural to urban areas for economic reasons, causing the growth of cities, or urbanization.

Earth's Human Geography

Directions: The underlined words in the following sentences are important key terms from Chapter 3. On the back of this page or on a separate sheet of paper, write sentences of your own using the terms or forms of the terms. If necessary, look up the terms in your textbook glossary.

1. The world's <u>population</u> was 3 billion in 1960. In the year 2000 it is expected to hit 6.4 billion.

2. <u>Population distribution</u> describes how the population is spread out over the Earth.

3. A <u>demographer</u> examines rates of birth, marriage, and death to learn about the world's populations.

4. <u>Population density</u> changes a great deal from place to place.

5. The <u>birthrate</u> in the United States has been increasing for many years.

6. Demographers can calculate population growth by comparing the birthrate and the <u>death rate</u>.

7. For many centuries, the <u>life expectancy</u> of the average person was short.

8. The <u>Green Revolution</u> has greatly increased the world's food supply.

9. When people move from one place to another, it is called <u>migration</u>.

10. Many Irish <u>immigrants</u> came to live in the cities of the northeastern United States during the 1840s and 1850s.

11. The <u>"push-pull" theory</u> is a way that demographers explain immigration.

12. <u>Urbanization</u> is a common trend in many parts of the world.

13. A <u>rural area</u> has a low population density.

14. The city of New York is an <u>urban area</u>.

Name _____ Class _____ Date _____

Earth's Human Geography

Directions: Use the information in Chapter 3 of your textbook to complete each statement.

1. People tend to settle in areas that

_____ .

2. The three continents on which more than 80 percent of the Earth's people live are

_____ .

3. Population growth depends on

_____ .

4. In modern times, the rate of growth of the world population has

_____ .

5. The life expectancy of people has increased in the last 100 years because

_____ .

6. The rapid growth of the world population has caused such problems as

_____ .

7. The "push-pull" theory states that people migrate because

_____ .

8. After the Vietnam War, many Vietnamese immigrated to the United States because

_____ .

9. In recent years, the populations of major cities throughout the world have grown a lot because

_____ .

10. Urbanization has resulted in such problems as

_____ .

© Prentice-Hall, Inc.

Earth's Human Geography

Feeding the World: Fish Farming

Directions: Read the passage and use the information to complete the cluster diagram.

As the world's population has grown, so has the demand for food. But some sources of food are rapidly disappearing. One of those sources is the supply of fish from the sea. Throughout the world, overfishing has nearly wiped out the populations of certain species of fish in areas where they were once common. The New England fishery is just one of many that have suffered. The populations of cod, haddock, and yellowtail flounder have sunk to record low levels off the coast of New England. Overfishing has also reduced the stocks of these fish along the coasts of Canada and countries that border the North Sea. Without close management, these species could completely disappear in some fisheries. To deal with the problem, fishing in many areas has been limited or outlawed to give the fish populations time to recover.

Another response to the problem has been the rise of fish farms, where fish are raised and sold, just like cattle and other livestock. On fish farms, fish are hatched and raised in tanks, ponds, or penned-in areas of a natural body of water. Species commonly raised on fish farms include shellfish, trout, salmon, catfish, and striped bass. Species of fish that live at least partly in freshwater are easier to raise. But fish farmers are experimenting with raising such saltwater species as halibut and flounder.

Fish farms create some of the same environmental problems that large livestock farms do, however. The heavy concentration of fish wastes from the farms can cause pollution. In Norway, for example, some fjords have been closed to swimming because of pollution from fish farms.

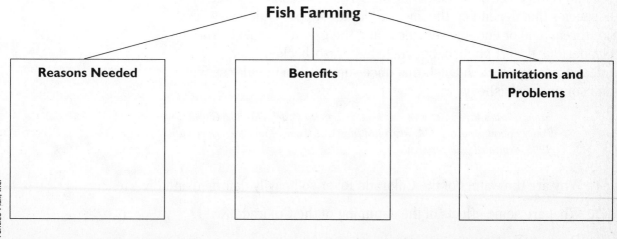

Fish Farming

Reasons Needed	**Benefits**	**Limitations and Problems**

CRITICAL THINKING

CHAPTER
3

Earth's Human Geography

Recognizing Cause and Effect

Running Out of Water

Directions: Read the following excerpt and answer the questions on another sheet of paper.

The Colorado River ranks among the most heavily plumbed water courses in the world. Controlled by 10 major dams, it irrigates some 2,000,000 acres of farmland, serves the household needs of more than 21,000,000 people, and generates nearly 12,000,000,000 kilowatt hours of energy annually. Its waters fill swimming pools and sprinkle green lawns some 250 miles away in Los Angeles, power neon lights in Las Vegas, and irrigate thirsty crops in the deserts of California, southern Arizona, and northern Mexico.

There are two major problems, though, with the way the Colorado was divided up decades ago. First, a total of 16,500,000 acre-feet (the volume of water that would cover one acre of land to the depth of one foot) was committed to seven U.S. states and Mexico, but the long-term average flow of the Colorado produces only about 90% of that—more water had been promised than the river reliably could deliver. Second, none of the compacts and treaties dividing up the Colorado's water designated any flow for the river environment itself, including the delta and its abundant wildlife. As long as human demands remained well below the river's flow, this was not a problem. However, except for unusually high flood years, virtually the entire flow of the river now is captured and used—and has been for some time…

Besides drying up wetlands and causing a severe deterioration in water quality, the reduction in freshwater has cut the flow of nutrients to the sea and reduced critical habitat for nursery grounds. A large number of species that depend on the lower Colorado–upper Gulf ecosystem are threatened or endangered, including the green sea turtle, Yuma clapper rail, desert pupfish, bonytail chub, razorback sucker, and totoaba, a large steel-blue fish that once supported a popular sports and commercial fishery.

From "Earth's Rivers Are Running Dry," by Sandra Postel, Director, Global Water Policy Project, Amherst, MA. Reprinted from USA Today Magazine, *November 1995. Reprinted with permission.*

1. Why are the waters of the Colorado River so heavily dammed and diverted?

2. What are some effects of the damming of the Colorado River?

© Prentice-Hall, Inc.

Cultures of the World

CHAPTER
4

Chapter and Section Support

Social Studies Hot Line

Dear Family,

We are now studying the cultures of the world as part of our continuing study of the Earth's geography. Your child will learn about differences and similarities between cultures throughout the world. We will explore the makeup of cultures, looking at social groups, language, and economic and political systems. We will also learn how cultures change, focusing on how most cultures in the world are changing very rapidly at this time.

Just talking about how families function in different ways will help prepare your child for the material in Chapter 4. You might talk with your child about your own experiences as a child or those of your parents and grandparents. You can compare the structures of families in the past with those of the present. These examples can illustrate changes that have taken place in your own experience. You could also explore together the experiences of your child's friends and their families.

We are surrounded by examples of cultural change. New words, technology, and ideas are introduced every day. Music comes to us from around the globe. Look for examples of how culture is changing in music, jobs, media, sports, or science. You might attend a science fair with your child or a museum of technology to find good examples.

I hope you and your child are continuing to enjoy sharing these explorations of the Earth and its geography.

Sincerely,

What Is Culture?

Lesson Objectives

Upon completion of this lesson, students will be able to
- define culture and describe its elements;
- explain how cultures are affected by their landscape and how they, in turn, affect their landscape;
- trace the early development of human culture.

Engage Motivate Students to Learn

Warm-Up Activity Write the following four headings on the chalkboard: *sports, foods, clothing,* and *entertainment.* Ask students to list, under each heading, things that are important parts of American life. Ask for specific items. Summarize by saying that these different parts of our way of life are only part of American culture.

Activating Prior Knowledge Have students read Reach Into Your Background in the Before You Read box. Invite students to discuss any customs or traditions they are familiar with that may be specific to another culture.

Explore Develop Main Ideas

Point out to students that geographers study how people affect their environment as well as how the environment affects people. Discuss how tools, fire, agriculture, and writing each contributed to the development of culture.

Teach Solicit Student Participation

Have students work in small groups to create a cause-and-effect graphic showing how the environment affects people living in their community. Direct students to list results or effects of each cause in a connecting box. Use the completed graphics to discuss how the local environment has shaped life in your community.

Assess Assess Evidence of Learning

See the answers to the Section Review questions. Students may also demonstrate evidence of learning by completing the Guided Reading and Review and the Section Quiz from the *Teaching Resources.* If students are doing a book project, this may also demonstrate evidence of learning by showing progress on project preparation.

CHAPTER 4
Cultures of
the World

What Is Culture?

A. As You Read

Directions: As you read Section 1, complete the statements below.

1. Geographers use levels of technology to see how _____ a culture is.

2. In Bali, Indonesia, people carved _____ into mountains to create farmland.

3. Before the Agricultural Revolution, people relied upon _____ for most of their food.

4. When people learned how to make and use fire, some people began living in areas with

   _____ climates.

5. A culture becomes a civilization when its people create a system of _____ to save knowledge and pass it on to others.

B. Reviewing Key Terms

Directions: In the blanks provided, write the definitions for the following key terms.

6. culture

_____

_____

7. cultural trait

_____

_____

8. technology

_____

_____

9. cultural landscape

_____

_____

10. agriculture

_____

_____

SECTION QUIZ

What Is Culture?

A. Key Terms and Concepts

Directions: Read the statements below. If a statement is true, write T in the blank provided. If it is false, write F. Rewrite false statements on another sheet of paper to make them true.

_____ **1.** Culture is the way of life of people who share different beliefs and customs.

_____ **2.** A group's cultural landscape includes any changes to its environment.

_____ **3.** A particular group's individual skills, customs, and ways of doing things are called individual characteristics.

_____ **4.** Technology refers to tools and the skills that people need to use them.

_____ **5.** Agriculture was an important part of the development of early cultures.

B. Main Ideas

Directions: Write the letter of the correct answer in each blank.

_____ **6.** Which of the following is a true statement about culture?
   a. Culture includes people's work, behavior, and beliefs.
   b. Culture often changes very quickly.
   c. Culture does not include material things.
   d. Language is not a part of culture.

_____ **7.** Which of the following might a geographer study to learn how landforms affect the culture of an area?
   a. how sports affect language
   b. how mountains affect farming
   c. how television affects families
   d. how the Internet affects literature

_____ **8.** In which environment would farmers be likely to make terraces for their farmland?
   a. wide, flat river valley
   b. the top of a plateau
   c. mountains
   d. low, flat plains

_____ **9.** How many stages do geographers say early cultures go through?
   a. two
   b. three
   c. four
   d. five

_____ **10.** A culture that creates a writing system is called a(n)
   a. technological society.
   b. traditional culture.
   c. agricultural society.
   d. civilization.

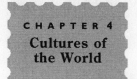

CHAPTER 4
Cultures of
the World

Social Groups,
Language, and Religion

Lesson Objectives

Upon completion of this lesson, students will be able to
- explain why social groups, language, and religion are important elements of every culture;
- describe how social groups, language, and religion make cultures differ from each other.

Engage Motivate Students to Learn

Warm-Up Activity Ask students why people live in families and why families are important. Then have them make lists of the kinds of things children learn from their families. Have the class share lists, and ask them to then add items they feel should be on their lists.

Activating Prior Knowledge Have students read Reach Into Your Background in the Before You Read box. Write students' other suggestions about culture on the chalkboard. Refer to the list as students read the section, editing or revising the list as needed.

Explore Develop Main Ideas

Have students read the section. Then ask the class to list the most important elements of cultures. Students should list families, other social organizations, language, and religion. With the class, create a chart that explains why a culture needs these elements to survive.

Teach Solicit Student Participation

Invite students to tell what they know about each of the following terms: *nuclear family, extended family,* and *social class.* Then, have them work in pairs to create their own definitions for the words. Suggest that as students read the section, they edit and revise their definitions and include examples of each term.

Assess Assess Evidence of Learning

See the answers to the Section Review questions. Students may also demonstrate evidence of learning by completing the Guided Reading and Review and the Section Quiz from the *Teaching Resources.* If students are doing a book project, this may also demonstrate evidence of learning by showing progress on project preparation.

GUIDED READING AND REVIEW

Social Groups, Language, and Religion

A. As You Read

Directions: As you read Section 2, fill in the table below with information about cultures.
Under each main idea, write two supporting statements.

Main Idea A
Each culture has its own social structure, or system of small groups within larger groups.
1. _____
2. _____

Main Idea B
Every culture is based on language.
3. _____
4. _____

B. Reviewing Key Terms

Directions: In the blanks provided, write the definitions for the following key terms.

5. social structure

_____

6. nuclear family

_____

7. extended family

_____

8. ethics

_____

CHAPTER 4
Cultures of
the World

Social Groups, Language, and Religion

A. Key Terms and Concepts

Directions: Match the definitions in Column I with the terms in Column II. Write the correct letter in each blank.

Column I

_____ 1. A family unit that includes a mother, a father, and their children is a(n) ____ .

_____ 2. Every culture has a(n) ____ , or way of organizing people into smaller groups.

_____ 3. Many cultures have ____ families, in which men make most of the decisions.

_____ 4. Religions guide people in their____ , or standards of correct, moral behavior.

_____ 5. Sometimes, several generations live together in a(n) ____ .

Column II

a. extended family

b. patriarchal

c. ethics

d. nuclear family

e. social structure

B. Main Ideas

Directions: Write the letter of the correct answer in each blank.

_____ 6. The most important social unit in a culture is the
    a. school.
    b. government.
    c. family.
    d. army.

_____ 7. Some cultures have matriarchal families in which
    a. fathers are in charge.
    b. mothers are in charge.
    c. grandfathers are in charge.
    d. teachers are in charge.

_____ 8. Social organization is important to a culture because it helps people
    a. learn about literature.
    b. travel to other places.
    c. learn about the geology of a place.
    d. work together to meet basic needs.

_____ 9. What are three important elements of a culture?
    a. food, clothing, and trade
    b. language, values, and religion
    c. values, geology and biology
    d. literature, geography, and trade

_____ 10. Which of the following is a true statement about language?
    a. Language helps people pass on what they know or believe to their children.
    b. People speak the same language in every country in the world.
    c. Language does not reflect what is important to people.
    d. The language of a country never changes.

Economic and Political Systems

Lesson Objectives

Upon completion of this lesson, students will be able to
- summarize the purpose of economic and political systems in cultures,
- compare and contrast the main types of economic and political systems.

Engage Motivate Students to Learn

Warm-Up Activity Discuss with students their answers to the following questions: What do they do when they want a glass of milk? How does milk get from the cow to their glass? Who owns the cows? Who owns the trucks or railroads that move the milk from one place to another? Elicit from students that some people choose to run farms that produce milk that they then sell directly to consumers. Similarly, help students recognize that many of the transportation systems are privately owned as well.

Activating Prior Knowledge Have students read Reach Into Your Background in the Before You Read box. Have students discuss what they know about voting and whether or not they think the same kind of voting occurs in other nations.

Explore Develop Main Ideas

Have students read the section. Then ask them to make a chart that identifies the roles of producers, consumers, and government in the economic systems of capitalism, socialism, and communism. Next, have students make an organizational chart comparing the hierarchies of power in a monarchy, a democracy, and a dictatorship.

Teach Solicit Student Participation

Organize students into six groups and assign each group one of the economic or political systems discussed in this section. Direct each group to prepare for a "press conference" about their topic. Class members can act as newspaper, magazine, or television reporters, asking group members about the principles, benefits, and disadvantages of their form of government or economic system. This activity should take about an hour.

Assess Assess Evidence of Learning

See the answers to the Section Review questions. Students may also demonstrate evidence of learning by completing the Guided Reading and Review and the Section Quiz from the *Teaching Resources*. If students are doing a book project, this may also demonstrate evidence of learning by showing progress on project preparation.

Name _____ Class _____ Date _____

Economic and Political Systems

A. As You Read

Directions: As you read Section 3, fill in the table below with details about the three basic economic systems.

Facts About Economic Systems

	Capitalism	Socialism	Communism
Who owns businesses?	1.	2.	3.
Who decides how much to pay workers and how to use profits?	4.	5.	6.

B. Reviewing Key Terms

Directions: Complete each sentence by writing the correct term(s) in the blank(s) provided.

7. When a king or a queen rules a government, the system is called a(n)

   _____ .

8. A system that sets up and enforces the laws of a society is called a(n)

   _____ .

9. A person who receives a good or service is called a(n) _____ .

10. In early governments, people lived in small groups and ran the day-to-day affairs of those groups. This form of government is called a(n) _____ .

11. The three basic economic systems are called _____ ,

    _____ , and _____ .

12. A person who has almost total control over a country is called a(n)

    _____ .

13. When citizens elect representatives to run a country, it is called a(n)

    _____ .

SECTION QUIZ

Economic and Political Systems

A. Key Terms and Concepts

Directions: Match the definitions in Column I with the terms in Column II. Write the correct letter in each blank.

Column I

_____ 1. a system in which people and privately owned companies own basic and nonbasic businesses

_____ 2. a ruler who has complete power over a country

_____ 3. a government in which the people participate directly in decision making

_____ 4. a person who buys goods and services

_____ 5. a system for producing, distributing, consuming, and owning goods, services, and wealth

Column II

a. direct democracy

b. capitalism

c. dictator

d. economy

e. consumer

B. Main Ideas

Directions: Write the letter of the correct answer in each blank.

_____ 6. What are the two types of products in any economy?
  a. computers and automobiles   c. farming and technology
  b. goods and services   d. businesses and technology

_____ 7. A basic business in an economic system might make
  a. sports equipment.   c. buses.
  b. compact discs.   d. running shoes.

_____ 8. What are the three basic economic systems?
  a. communism, democracy, and   c. communism, capitalism,
     capitalism   and socialism
  b. socialism, absolute monarchy, d. consumerism, capitalism,
     and dictatorship   and monarchy

_____ 9. The system that sets up and enforces a society's laws and institutions is called the
  a. monarchy.   c. economy.
  b. government.   d. technology.

_____ 10. In a representative democracy, citizens elect representatives who create
  a. a monarchy.   c. laws.
  b. the culture's language.   d. new technology.

CHAPTER 4
Cultures of
the World

Cultural Change

Lesson Objectives

Upon completion of this lesson, students will be able to
- summarize reasons why cultures change,
- explain why cultures are changing rapidly today,
- evaluate the benefits and problems of rapid cultural change.

Engage Motivate Students to Learn

Warm-Up Activity Encourage students to list things Americans have today that we did not have 50 years ago. Compile a list on the chalkboard. Ask students to identify which items people in other parts of the world also have.

Activating Prior Knowledge Have students read Reach Into Your Background in the Before You Read box. List students' suggestions concerning types of music that show a cultural blend.

Explore Develop Main Ideas

Have students read the section. Work with the class to create a chart titled *Cultural Change* with these headings: *Natural Environment, Technological Changes,* and *New Ideas.* Ask the class for examples of how each has changed cultures. Discuss cultural diffusion and acculturation and ask for examples. Ask students why cultural change can sometimes be negative.

Teach Solicit Student Participation

After students have read the chapter, suggest that they form two competing quiz show teams. Each team prepares answers for the opposing team using key terms and main ideas presented in the section. Teams, in turn, respond to the answers by providing the question appropriate to the answer. If a "contestant" cannot respond, or responds incorrectly, the team loses a turn. Correct answers get one point each.

Assess Assess Evidence of Learning

See the answers to the Section Review questions. Students may also demonstrate evidence of learning by completing the Guided Reading and Review and the Section Quiz from the *Teaching Resources.* If students are doing a book project, this may also demonstrate evidence of learning by showing progress on project preparation.

Name _____ Class _____ Date _____

Cultural Change

A. As You Read

Directions: As you read Section 4, answer the following questions in the space provided.

1. What are some things that can affect culture?

_____

_____

2. How does the story about jeans explain cultural diffusion?

_____

_____

3. What is an example of acculturation in sports today?

_____

_____

4. How has new technology sped up the process of cultural change?

_____

_____

5. Why do some people refer to the Earth as a "global village"?

_____

_____

6. How have cultures changed in relation to the environment?

_____

_____

B. Reviewing Key Terms

Directions: In the blanks provided, write the definitions for the following key terms.

7. cultural diffusion

_____

_____

8. acculturation

_____

_____

CHAPTER 4
Cultures of
the World

Cultural Change

A. Key Terms and Concepts

Directions: Read the statements below. If a statement is true, write T in the blank provided. If it is false, write F. Rewrite false statements on another sheet of paper to make them true.

_____ **1.** The movement of customs from one culture to another is called cultural change.

_____ **2.** Acculturation is the process of borrowing trade routes among cultures.

_____ **3.** Today, many people call the Earth a "global village."

_____ **4.** New ideas can change a culture.

_____ **5.** If things in a culture change too slowly, people can become confused and the culture is threatened.

B. Main Ideas

Directions: Write the letter of the correct answer in each blank.

_____ **6.** A change in the climate of a place can change a culture by affecting
   a. acculturation.
   b. the food people grow.
   c. its ancient history.
   d. the global village.

_____ **7.** The worldwide concern about the environment that began in the 1950s is an example of a(n)
   a. information overload.
   b. environmental change.
   c. cultural change.
   d. technological change.

_____ **8.** Sending a space shuttle into orbit is one example of how
   a. technology changes our culture.
   b. customs change our culture.
   c. weather changes our culture.
   d. geology changes our culture.

_____ **9.** As a result of recent technological advancements, cultural change has
   a. slowed.
   b. affected very few people.
   c. not affected people.
   d. sped up.

_____ **10.** Why are people working to save their own cultures?
   a. to create new inventions
   b. to keep valuable traditions from being lost
   c. to save their environments
   d. to protect technological advancements

CHAPTER SUMMARY

Cultures of the World

Guiding Question:
- What is a culture?

Culture is the way of life of a group of people who share similar customs, beliefs, and ideas. Geographers want to know how landforms, climate, vegetation, and resources affect culture. These effects are part of the theme of human-environment interaction.

Early cultures developed over long periods of time. Geographers divide the development of early cultures into these stages: inventing tools, discovering fire, developing agriculture, and using writing.

Every culture has a social structure, or a way of organizing people into smaller groups with particular tasks. Families are the most important social unit of any culture. Children learn from their families the customs and traditions of their culture. In some cultures, the basic family unit is the nuclear family, or a mother, a father, and their children. In other cultures, the basic unit is the extended family, which includes people from several generations living in one place. Language is another very important part of culture. It lets people communicate everything they need to share in their culture.

There are several different types of economic systems. These include capitalism, socialism, and communism. There are also different types of political systems, including direct democracy, representative democracy, monarchy, and dictatorship. In each system, the control of goods, services, wealth, and power is divided in some way between the government and its citizens.

Many factors, such as new ideas, technology, and migrations of people, can cause a culture to change. In recent years, cultural change has been taking place more and more quickly. One important change has been in modern communications, which connect people, businesses, and governments from nearby or far away almost instantly. However, rapid change can be destructive. Modern technology often replaces older sources of knowledge, which can be lost forever. Many people are working today to preserve important elements of their cultures.

VOCABULARY ACTIVITY

Cultures of the World

CHAPTER
4

Directions: Match the definitions in Column I with the key terms in Column II. Write the correct letter in each blank. If necessary, look up the terms in your textbook glossary.

Column I

_____ **1.** a system of government in which the people participate directly in decision making

_____ **2.** a system of government in which a king or a queen rules

_____ **3.** a set of laws that define a government's power

_____ **4.** work done for other people, such as the work of a doctor

_____ **5.** farming

_____ **6.** the system that establishes and enforces the laws and institutions of a society

_____ **7.** the ways in which people within a culture are organized into smaller groups

_____ **8.** government system in which people elect representatives to run national affairs

_____ **9.** products that are made to be sold, such as cars

_____ **10.** a behavioral characteristic of a people, such as a language, passed on to each generation

_____ **11.** a system for producing, distributing, consuming, and owning goods, services, and wealth

_____ **12.** a landscape that has been changed by people, reflecting their culture

_____ **13.** an economic system in which the government owns all businesses and industries

_____ **14.** the way of life of a people who share beliefs

_____ **15.** an economic system in which people and privately owned companies own most basic and nonbasic businesses and industries

_____ **16.** an economic system in which the government owns most basic industries; nonbasic industries are privately owned

Column II

a. socialism

b. agriculture

c. capitalism

d. communism

e. constitution

f. cultural landscape

g. cultural trait

h. culture

i. direct democracy

j. economy

k. goods

l. government

m. monarchy

n. representative democracy

o. services

p. social structure

Name _____ Class _____ Date _____

Cultures of the World

Directions: Use the information in Chapter 4 of your textbook to fill in the outline. Write a brief description for each topic on the back of this page or on another sheet of paper.

I. What Is Culture?

   A. Definition of culture and cultural traits

   B. What geographers want to know about culture

   C. Major stages in the development of early cultures

II. Social Groups, Language, and Religion

   A. The basic social unit of societies

   B. Importance of language to social groups

   C. Importance of religion in a culture

III. Economic and Political Systems

   A. Types of economic systems

   B. Forms of government

IV. Cultural Change

   A. Things that cause cultures to change

   B. Effects of the increased rate of cultural change

Name_____ Class_____ Date_____

Cultures of the World

Cultural Diffusion: The Spread of Wheat-Growing

Directions: The map shows how wheat-growing spread throughout the world from an area in the Middle East called the Fertile Crescent. Study the map and answer the questions.

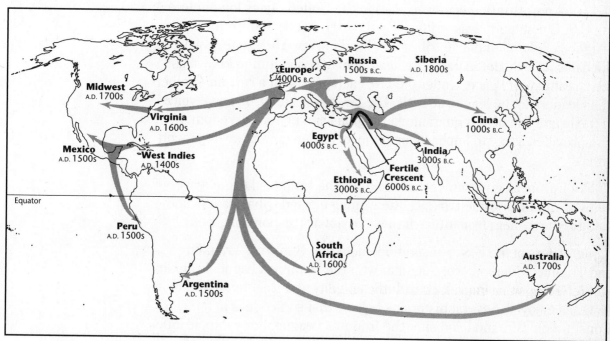

1. Describe how wheat-growing spread from the Fertile Crescent.

_____

_____

_____

2. How long did it take for wheat-growing to spread from the Fertile Crescent to Siberia?

_____

3. The spread of wheat-growing throughout the world is an example of how cultural practices spread slowly long ago. How long do you think it would take for a new farm product or practice to spread throughout the world today? Why?

_____

_____

Based on a map from THE WORLD BOOK ENCYCLOPEDIA © 1994 World Book, Inc. By permission of the publisher.

CRITICAL THINKING

CHAPTER
4

Cultures of the World

Making Comparisons

The Great Law of Peace

Directions: Read the passage about the government of the Iroquois League, a political union of Native American tribes. Use the information and your own knowledge about the original U.S. Constitution to complete the activities.

Did you know that democracy existed in the United States long before the U.S. Constitution was written? By the early 1600s, the Iroquois League, a federation of five tribes that lived in New York state, practiced the basic ideas of democracy. The league had a constitution known as the Great Law of Peace. Under the law, each tribe sent a certain number of its leaders to the league council. The law gave each tribe equal voice in the league council. It guaranteed religious and political freedom. It also provided a way to impeach, or remove, leaders and a way to amend laws.

Unlike European governments of the time, the Iroquois League gave political rights to women. In fact, the women elected tribal leaders and could remove them from office if they did not act responsibly.

Some writers of the U.S. Constitution, including Benjamin Franklin and Thomas Jefferson, were familiar with the Iroquois League. Franklin and Jefferson were impressed with the equality and freedom that the Iroquois enjoyed. Several historians believe that some ideas in the U.S. Constitution were modeled after the Iroquois League. For example, our federation of states may have been patterned after the federation of tribes in the Iroquois League.

1. What are some similarities and differences between the Iroquois League and the original U.S. Constitution?

   _____

   _____

   _____

   _____

2. Find out more about the Great Law of Peace of the Iroquois League. Write a short essay describing other similarities and differences between it and the original U.S. Constitution.

Name _____ Class _____ Date _____

Earth's Natural Resources

Social Studies Hot Line

Dear Family,

As our social studies class completes its study of world geography, we will explore the Earth's natural resources and how they are used. We will also learn about how people affect their environment. As we learned in Chapter 4, the rapidly expanding world population is exerting a great pressure on the world's natural resources. You can begin to discuss this issue with your child by talking about the value of recycling and using recycled products.

Part of our study in Chapter 5 will include learning about renewable natural resources such as trees and crops, and nonrenewable natural resources such as oil and minerals. As you listen to or watch the news with your child, you might point out stories about different types of resources. If you have recently taken a trip or driven around your local area, you can talk about land use. Do you live in a rural, agricultural area? Are you in an urban area where the land is covered with structures?

A look around your house can inspire a discussion with your child of the stages of economic activity. Where do the products in your house come from? Are there any that are the direct result of your labor, such as fish you caught or objects you made? Are there products that were made by someone you know in your community? Which products come from other places through a distributor?

Encourage your child to cut out news articles about pollution and its effect on the environment. You might talk about places where you have noticed pollution in the air, the soil, or bodies of water in and around your community.

I hope you have enjoyed this study of the Earth's geography. Your help is greatly appreciated as we work together with your child.

Sincerely,

What Are Natural Resources?

Lesson Objectives

Upon completion of this lesson, students will be able to
- identify natural resources and trace the operations through which raw materials are processed for human use,
- differentiate between renewable and nonrenewable natural resources,
- describe fossil fuel energy resources and patterns of consumption.

Engage Motivate Students to Learn

Warm-Up Activity Ask students to identify an object in the classroom that is in its natural form. Then, have the students name the raw materials used to make several classroom objects.

Activating Prior Knowledge Have students read Reach Into Your Background in the Before You Read box. Encourage students to keep a list of everything they throw out in a day.

Explore Develop Main Ideas

Direct students to read the section. Encourage them to look for answers to questions such as these: Why do people need natural resources? How are some natural resources changed before they are used? What happens if a renewable resource is not replaced? Why is it a good idea to use recycled materials? Why have people started looking for new energy resources?

Teach Solicit Student Participation

Have students identify the basic materials they see around them in the classroom and create a chart with the following column headings:
- Item
- Wood, Metal, or Plastic
- Renewable or Nonrenewable Resource
- Recyclable or Nonrecyclable
- Energy Resources Used to Produce

Ask students to indicate whether each item is from a renewable resource and whether it can be recycled or not. Then have them describe the energy resources that were used to produce each item. Use completed charts for discussion. This activity should take about 30 minutes.

Assess Assess Evidence of Learning

See the answers to the Section Review questions. Students may also demonstrate evidence of learning by completing the Guided Reading and Review and the Section Quiz from the *Teaching Resources*. If students are doing a book project, this may also demonstrate evidence of learning by showing progress on project preparation.

CHAPTER 5
Earth's Natural Resources

What Are Natural Resources?

A. As You Read

Directions: As you read Section 1, fill in the chart below with information about natural resources.

Original Resource	Type of Resource	Possible Uses
Tree	1.	2.
Corn	3.	4.
Water	5.	6.
Natural Gas	7.	8.

B. Reviewing Key Terms

Directions: In the blanks provided, write the definitions for the following key terms.

9. natural resource

_____

_____

10. raw material

_____

_____

11. recyclable resource

_____

_____

12. renewable resource

_____

13. nonrenewable resource

_____

14. fossil fuel

_____

_____

SECTION QUIZ

What Are Natural Resources?

A. Key Terms and Concepts

Directions: Fill in the blanks in Column I with the terms in Column II. Write the correct letter in each blank.

Column I

_____ 1. A resource in its natural state is a _____ .

_____ 2. Any useful material found in the environment is a _____ .

_____ 3. When a _____ , such as oil, is used up, it cannot be replaced.

_____ 4. A material that can be replaced after it is used is called a _____ .

_____ 5. A material that cycles through natural processes in the environment is a _____ .

Column II

a. raw material

b. recyclable resource

c. nonrenewable resource

d. natural resource

e. renewable resource

B. Main Ideas

Directions: Write the letter of the correct answer in each blank.

_____ 6. Anything from the Earth that helps to meet people's needs for food, clothing, or shelter is a
   a. landform.
   b. culture.
   c. resource.
   d. fossil.

_____ 7. Geographers call water a
   a. nonrenewable resource.
   b. recyclable resource.
   c. raw material.
   d. synthetic resource.

_____ 8. Which of the following is an example of indirect energy use?
   a. a clock that runs on electricity
   b. a car that uses gasoline
   c. a plastic broom made in a factory
   d. a furnace that uses natural gas

_____ 9. Over millions of years, the remains of prehistoric plants and animals have created
   a. renewable resources.
   b. recyclable resources.
   c. synthetic fuels.
   d. fossil fuels.

_____ 10. Which of the following is a true statement about the world's energy resources?
   a. All countries have the same amounts of oil, coal, and natural gas.
   b. Energy resources are not evenly spread around the world.
   c. It is not necessary to find more sources of energy.
   d. In 1973, countries in the Middle East decided to sell more of their oil.

© Prentice-Hall, Inc.

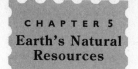

CHAPTER 5
Earth's Natural
Resources

How People Use the Land

Lesson Objectives

Upon completion of this lesson, students will be able to
- identify stages of economic development and describe some of the problems faced at each stage;
- compare and contrast ways different cultures use land and other resources;
- describe patterns of economic activity on a global scale, including the relationship between developed and developing countries.

Engage Motivate Students to Learn

Warm-Up Activity Help students recognize that one of the most important natural resources is human labor. As an example, ask students to describe a favorite meal. Ask them who worked to make the food, including everyone along the way, from the farmer, the worker in the manufacturing plant, the packer, the trucker, the grocery store clerks, and the cooks. Then ask them to summarize the human resources used to make their meal.

Activating Prior Knowledge Have students read Reach Into Your Background in the Before You Read box. Most students' lists will include resources such as metal, plants, and animals.

Explore Develop Main Ideas

As they read the section, have students consider the following questions. Who works directly with natural resources? Who works with changing raw materials into goods? Why do both service and manufacturing industries rely on natural resources? Why are there conflicts between small farmers and big industries? Why don't developing countries use modern technology?

Teach Solicit Student Participation

Ask students to choose a familiar manufactured product—a CD or a video game, for example—and figure out the raw materials, manufacturing processes, and service tasks that moved that product from natural resources to its daily use. Have students create a diagram that shows all of the human and natural resources involved in producing the product. Use the diagrams as a basis for discussion of the relationship between economic activity and resource use. This activity should take about 40 minutes.

Assess Assess Evidence of Learning

See the answers to the Section Review questions. Students may also demonstrate evidence of learning by completing the Guided Reading and Review and the Section Quiz from the *Teaching Resources.* If students are doing a book project, it may also demonstrate evidence of learning by showing progress on project preparation.

Name _____ Class _____ Date _____

How People Use the Land

A. As You Read

Directions: As you read Section 2, answer the following questions in the space provided.

1. In which stage of economic activity do people turn raw materials into things they use?

_____

2. What happened during the Industrial Revolution?

_____

3. What types of things can stop the movement of goods and services from one country to another?

_____

4. What are some challenges that developing nations face?

_____

B. Reviewing Key Terms

Directions: Complete each sentence by writing the correct term in the blank provided.

5. Farming done on large farms owned by companies instead of single families is called

_____ .

6. The governments of developed countries often give loans, or _____ ,
to the governments of developing nations.

7. When farmers grow only enough food to feed their own families, they practice

_____ .

8. A commercial farm that employs many workers but is owned by only a few people

is called a(n) _____ .

9. A country that has few industries is called a(n) _____ nation, whereas

a country with many industries is called a(n) _____ nation.

10. The process of changing a raw material into a finished product is known as

_____ .

CHAPTER 5
Earth's Natural
Resources

How People Use the Land

A. Key Terms and Concepts

Directions: Match the definitions in Column I with the terms in Column II. Write the correct letter in each blank.

Column I

_____ 1. a modern industrial society

_____ 2. farming that is done by companies

_____ 3. the process of turning a raw material into a finished product

_____ 4. a large farm that raises a single crop for export

_____ 5. economic and military aid to another country

Column II

a. manufacturing

b. plantation

c. foreign aid

d. commercial farming

e. developed nation

B. Main Ideas

Directions: Write the letter of the correct answer in each blank.

_____ 6. Turning raw materials into things that people can use is the
    a. first stage of economic development.
    b. second stage of economic development.
    c. third stage of economic development.
    d. fourth stage of economic development.

_____ 7. Which of the following is an example of a first-level economic activity?
    a. manufacturing
    b. distribution
    c. herding
    d. processing

_____ 8. The Industrial Revolution separated the world's countries into
    a. northern and southern nations.
    b. developed and developing nations.
    c. western and eastern nations.
    d. ancient and modern nations.

_____ 9. Many people in developing nations get their food by practicing
    a. subsistence farming.
    b. commercial farming.
    c. plantation farming.
    d. developing farming.

_____ 10. Most of the people of the world live in
    a. North and South America.
    b. the United States.
    c. developed nations.
    d. developing nations.

People's Effect on the Environment

Lesson Objectives

Upon completion of this lesson, students will be able to
- summarize some of the ways in which people's actions affect the environment,
- describe actions taken to protect endangered species and ecosystems,
- identify energy sources that can be used in place of fossil fuels.

Engage Motivate Students to Learn

Warm-Up Activity Have students describe a park they are familiar with. Ask them to describe the grasses, plants, bushes, and trees they find there. Are there many kinds of plants? What things in the park were put there by humans? What would happen to the trees and wildlife if the park were to be used as an airport?

Activating Prior Knowledge Have students read Reach Into Your Background in the Before You Read box. If students aren't aware of local environmental issues, you might suggest that they look for information in the local newspaper. Encourage students to think about actions they can take to improve the environment, such as recycling, putting litter in its place, helping to plant trees, and so on.

Explore Develop Main Ideas

As students read the section, suggest that they look for answers to these questions: Why is it important to plant trees? Why is deforestation a problem? How does industry contribute to environmental problems? Why are ultraviolet rays from the sun more of a problem now than they were 100 years ago? How does burning fossil fuels contribute to pollution?

Teach Solicit Student Participation

Have students make a chart to organize the information in the text. Possible column heads might include *Problems* and *Possible Solutions*. Subjects might include air, water, plants, and animals. Opinions can be included in the chart when supported by fact. Use the completed charts as a basis for discussion on environmental problems. This activity should take about 40 minutes.

Assess Assess Evidence of Learning

See the answers to the Section Review questions. Students may also demonstrate evidence of learning by completing the Guided Reading and Review and the Section Quiz from the *Teaching Resources*. If students are doing a book project, this may also demonstrate evidence of learning by showing progress on project preparation.

© Prentice-Hall, Inc.

Name _____ Class _____ Date _____

CHAPTER 5
Earth's Natural
Resources

People's Effect
on the Environment

A. As You Read

Directions: As you read Section 3, fill in the table below with information about people and the environment. Under each main idea, write two supporting statements.

Main Idea A
Living things are tied to their ecosystems, and certain changes can destroy those ecosystems.

1. _____

_____

2. _____

_____

Main Idea B
Many countries and organizations are making efforts to reduce the use of things that are harmful to the environment.

3. _____

_____

4. _____

_____

B. Reviewing Key Terms

Directions: Complete each sentence by writing the correct term in the blank provided.

5. One way to prevent an endangered species from dying out is to defend the environment

it lives in, or its _____ .

6. A layer of gas in the upper atmosphere called the _____ blocks most of the harmful ultraviolet rays from the sun.

7. Most American city governments encourage people to _____ many used materials such as newspapers, bottles, and cans.

8. When chemicals combine with water vapor in the air, they form _____ .

9. The release of greenhouse gases in the air may be the cause of _____ .

SECTION QUIZ

People's Effect on the Environment

A. Key Terms and Concepts

Directions: Read the statements below. If a statement is true, write T in the blank provided. If it is false, write F. Rewrite false statements on another sheet of paper to make them true.

_____ **1.** A community of living things and its environment is called a habitat.

_____ **2.** The ozone layer is a layer of gas in the upper part of the atmosphere.

_____ **3.** To recycle is to use only new materials to make new products.

_____ **4.** The process of clearing land of trees is called forestation.

_____ **5.** Global warming is a slow increase in the Earth's temperature due to the increasing amount of carbon dioxide in the atmosphere.

B. Main Ideas

Directions: Write the letter of the correct answer in each blank.

_____ **6.** Which of the following is an example of an ecosystem?
   a. an endangered species
   b. the Amazon River Valley
   c. the Washington Monument
   d. a blade of grass

_____ **7.** What is the goal of the Endangered Species Act?
   a. to protect important landforms
   b. to encourage the creation of new plant life
   c. to stop the extinction of plants and animals
   d. to encourage people to reuse natural resources

_____ **8.** Acid rain is caused by the use of
   a. fossil fuels.
   b. nuclear power.
   c. aerosol spray cans.
   d. solar energy.

_____ **9.** Which of the following energy sources is an alternative to fossil fuels?
   a. coal
   b. natural gas
   c. oil
   d. wind

_____ **10.** In the 1970s, scientists realized that chlorofluorocarbons (CFCs) were destroying
   a. forests in New York.
   b. the ozone layer.
   c. the Amazon Rain Forest.
   d. the fossil fuel supply.

Earth's Natural Resources

Guiding Question:

- How do people use the world's resources?

Natural resources are any useful materials found in the environment, such as water, minerals, soil, and vegetation. Natural resources are used for many things, including food, fuel, clothing, and shelter. There are three types of resources. Recyclable resources are those, such as water, that cycle naturally through the environment. Renewable resources are those that can be replaced, such as trees. Nonrenewable resources, such as oil and coal, cannot be replaced once they are used up.

Geographers have identified three stages of resource use. In the first stage, people use land and resources directly to make products. They may hunt, cut wood, mine, and fish. In the second stage, people turn raw materials into products through manufacturing. In the third stage, people provide a service rather than a product. They distribute products they have not made themselves.

There are two major categories of countries in the world today: developed and developing countries. Developed countries have many industries, while developing countries have few. Most people in developed nations live in towns or cities. Many people in developing nations live in rural areas and make a living by farming or herding animals.

Ecosystems are places where living and nonliving things depend upon each other for survival. Deserts, rain forests, and grasslands are some examples of ecosystems. If one part of an ecosystem changes, other parts are also affected. Some human activities, such as the deforestation of the rain forests in South America, can destroy an ecosystem. Pollution from factories and automobiles can cause acid rain, damage water systems, and destroy the ozone layer. To solve these problems, scientists are looking for less-polluting sources of energy. They are researching new ways to use nuclear power, water, wind, and the sun for energy.

Name _____ Class _____ _____ Date _____

Earth's Natural Resources

Directions: Below is a list of key terms from Chapter 5. Write one sentence or phrase that uses each term on a separate sheet of paper. If necessary, look in Chapter 5 to see how the terms are used.

1. **natural resource**—any useful material from the environment that humans use to survive

2. **raw material**—a resource that is still in its natural state

3. **recyclable resource**—a resource that cycles through natural processes in the environment

4. **renewable resource**—a natural resource that the environment replaces as it is used

5. **nonrenewable resource**—a resource that cannot be replaced once it is used

6. **fossil fuel**—a resource created from the remains of plants and animals

7. **manufacturing**—the process of turning a raw material into a finished product

8. **developed nation**—a modern industrial society with a well-developed economy

9. **developing nation**—a country with relatively low industrial production

10. **commercial farming**—farming that is done by companies

11. **subsistence farming**—farming that provides only enough food for a family or village

12. **plantation**—a large estate on which crops are grown by workers living there

13. **foreign aid**—economic and military aid to another country

14. **ecosystem**—a community of living things and its environment

15. **deforestation**—the process of clearing land of forests or trees

16. **habitat**—the area in which a plant or an animal naturally grows or lives

17. **acid rain**—rain whose high level of chemicals can pollute the environment

18. **ozone layer**—a layer of gas in the upper atmosphere that blocks most of the sun's harmful rays

19. **global warming**—a slow increase in the Earth's temperature

20. **recycle**—to reuse materials to make new products

Name _____ Class _____ Date _____

RETEACHING

CHAPTER 5

Chapter and Section Support

Earth's Natural Resources

Directions: Use the information in Chapter 5 of your textbook to describe each item. Include an example of each.

1. a renewable natural resource _____

_____

2. a nonrenewable natural resource _____

_____

3. a recyclable natural resource _____

_____

4. a fossil fuel _____

_____

5. a first-level economic activity _____

_____

6. a second-level economic activity _____

_____

7. a third-level economic activity _____

_____

8. a characteristic of a developed nation _____

_____

9. a challenge for a developing nation _____

_____

10. a result of deforestation _____

11. an effect of acid rain _____

12. a source of water pollution _____

13. a possible cause of global warming _____

14. an alternative energy source to fossil fuels _____

_____

15. a way to protect the environment _____

_____

© Prentice-Hall, Inc.

Earth's Natural Resources

Chapter and Section Resources ■ 77

ENRICHMENT

CHAPTER 5

Earth's Natural Resources

Owls and Jobs

Directions: Read the excerpt about the aftermath of a struggle over natural resources that pitted environmentalists against loggers in Oregon. Then complete one of the activities.

Having Owls and Jobs Too

Sawing down 200-year-old trees was just about the only thing former logger John Dark ever wanted to do. Working in the woods was a dream job for the Oregon native. There were good wages, fresh air and the incredible [excitement] of toppling Douglas firs without [ruining] 4,000 board feet of lumber. . . .

Then, in 1991, U.S. District Judge William Dwyer declared [an end to] cutting old-growth-forest habitat that is critical for the northern spotted owl. And Dark lost his job . . . a victim of what has been dubbed the "owl wars." But his story does not end there. Like 4,340 of his former colleagues since 1989, Dark [chose] formal retraining. He enrolled in business and accounting classes in a mostly federally funded program at a community college near his home in Creswell. The 32-year-old student now plans to build and market [fancy] wooden dollhouses he has designed. And he says, "Getting laid off was the best thing that ever happened to me."

The optimism of Dark and other former timber-industry workers about finding a place in Oregon's changing economy is shared by [many] economists, state officials and timber-industry analysts. Since Dwyer's ruling four years ago, the Oregon economy has [proved wrong those] who swore the economy would collapse and mill towns would become ghost towns. . . .

. . . Other forest industries are emerging that can profit without making stumps out of centuries-old trees. Catherine Mater, president of Corvallis-based Mater Engineering, estimates that [growing flowers] for the international floral industry could bring in $72 million per year.

Former mill towns like Oakridge, which is surrounded by the Willamette National Forest, are promoting . . . products that in some way create other jobs, such as making locally produced flower boxes from locally harvested scrap cedar. "We have a lot to learn about how to use the resources we have available to us," Mater says. "The timing is so ripe to look at alternatives. . . ."

Meanwhile, . . . other positive trends have emerged from the owl wars. One example, says Bob Warren of the Oregon governor's forest-policy team, is a recent "[huge] leap in forest management."

Clear-cutting has decreased, and no-cut buffer areas around streams are commonplace, though some critics charge that they are still inadequate. The industry has become more efficient and innovative.

From "Having Owls and Jobs Too," by Daniel Glick, National Wildlife Magazine, *August-September 1995. Reprinted with the permission of* National Wildlife Magazine.

Activities

- What new type of business would you start if you were a logger who lost your job in Oregon? Write a short business plan describing your business.
- Use the information from this excerpt to write a script for a radio news story about the aftermath of the "owl wars" in Oregon.

Earth's Natural Resources

Identifying Central Issues

Saving the Mountain Gorilla

Directions: Read the passage. Then complete the chart identifying problems and solutions in the conservation effort to save the mountain gorilla.

Wildlife is one of the world's resources that is rapidly shrinking due to the demands of a growing human population. The mountain gorilla is one example of this dwindling resource. The Bwindi-Impenetrable Forest in the highlands of Uganda is home to 300 mountain gorillas, half of the world population of these apes. Despite the fact that these animals live in a protected park, they are far from safe. At the park's edge is a growing population of people with many needs. For generations, the local people have depended on the forests in the park for firewood, foods, medicines, and income from illegal gorilla-poaching and timber-cutting.

Local and international conservation groups have realized that the support of the local people is needed to save the gorillas. So they began programs to gain that support. To make up for the loss of income from illegal poaching and timber-cutting, conservationists now use the gorillas as tourist bait to earn money for the local community. Tourists pay a fee to enter the park, and the money is used to fund community projects. In addition, local people have been hired and trained as conservation agents who teach farmers ways to improve their crop yields. For example, the agents encourage farmers to plant trees along the edges of their fields, which improves the soil fertility, prevents erosion, and also provides firewood. A "multiple-use program" has also been instituted for the park. It allows local people to harvest controlled amounts of medicinal plants as well as honey from the forests.

Efforts to Save the Mountain Gorilla

Problems	Solutions
1.	2.
3.	4.
5.	6.

Answer Key

Chapter 1

Section 1 Guided Reading

1. "Where are things located?" and "Why are they there?"
2. They help geographers to organize information.
3. absolute location and relative location
4. relative location
5. It helps them understand the relationship among places.
6. geography
7. parallel, latitude
8. meridian, longitude
9. Prime Meridian
10. Equator
11. degree

Section 1 Quiz

1. T
2. F; Lines of latitude circle the Earth parallel to the Equator.
3. T
4. T
5. F; Lines of latitude divide the globe into units called degrees.
6. c   7. b   8. d   9. b   10. a

Section 2 Guided Reading

1. Maps showed only areas where people traveled. Sometimes, places were left out of maps.
2. People sometimes filled empty spaces in maps with drawings of mythical lands, creatures, and people from stories.
3. Maps are easier to carry than globes.
4. A folded map can show many details of communities, cities, and states. A globe would need to be very large to show the same kind of detailed information.
5. distortion
6. key
7. globe, scale
8. projection
9. rose, cardinal directions

Section 2 Quiz

1. d   2. e   3. b   4. c   5. a
6. c   7. d   8. a   9. c   10. a

Vocabulary Activity

Sentences will vary. Sample answers are given.

1. The cardinal direction north is found on most maps.
2. Most maps include a compass rose, which shows the cardinal directions.
3. There are 15 degrees between each longitude line on our classroom map of the world.
4. The Mercator projection map contains a distortion that makes Greenland look bigger than South America.
5. The distance between the Equator and the North and South poles is the same.
6. The five themes of geography are location, place, human-environment interaction, movement, and regions.
7. Because it is round, a globe is the best way to represent the shapes and sizes of the continents and oceans of the Earth.
8. When you don't understand a map symbol, look it up in the key.
9. The Tropic of Cancer is a latitude line that circles the globe 23.45 degrees north of the Equator.
10. Longitude lines help navigators know how far east or west they are from a certain point.
11. *Meridian* is another term for longitude line.
12. The reason that latitude lines are called parallels is because they are parallel to each other and never meet.
13. Some maps show whether a certain area is a plain, a mountain, or other landform.
14. Geographers measure locations east or west of the Prime Meridian.
15. The Mercator projection map has been used by deep-sea navigators for hundreds of years.

Answer Key

16. Our class has a map of California with a scale of 1 inch = 100 miles.

Reteaching

Students' examples will vary, but should demonstrate knowledge of the meaning of each theme.

1. e
2. c
3. a
4. b
5. d

Enrichment

1. The two maps both show the continents of Europe, Asia, and Africa and the oceans surrounding these continents.
2. The map of 1490 does not show the continents of North America, South America, Australia, or Antarctica. The sizes and shapes of Asia and Africa are very different. The map of 1490 lacks lines of latitude and longitude, a scale, a compass rose, and a key.
3. the Western Hemisphere, especially Europe
4. Answers will vary.

Critical Thinking

1. forest and grassland
2. growing crops and grazing livestock
3. growing crops and grazing livestock
4. They were cut down to make way for farms and ranches.
5. Human beings have drastically changed the vegetation over much of the land in the United States.

Chapter 2

Section 1 Guided Reading

1. The lights from its many stars look like spilled milk across the sky.
2. because the Earth's axis is at an angle
3. June 20 or 21
4. Locations in the tropics receive direct sunlight.
5. axis
6. high
7. middle
8. orbit
9. rotation
10. revolution
11. low

Section 1 Quiz

1. e **2.** d **3.** a **4.** c **5.** b
6. b **7.** c **8.** c **9.** d **10.** a

Section 2 Guided Reading

1. The different continents look as though they might fit together like the pieces of a puzzle.
2. Scientists in the 1960s found fossil evidence that supported the concept of Pangaea.
3. Florida's plate moves to the west, moving it farther away from Europe about an inch every year.
4. When different plates push against each other, pressure builds and volcanoes develop.
5. mountain, hill
6. plain
7. plateau
8. landform
9. plate
10. plate tectonics

Section 2 Quiz

1. T
2. F; According to the theory of plate tectonics, the Earth's crust is broken into huge pieces called plates.
3. F; The breaking down of rocks by wind, rain, and ice is called weathering.
4. T
5. T

6. c **7.** b **8.** a **9.** c **10.** d

Answer Key

Section 3 Guided Reading

1. weather
2. ocean currents
3. cooler
4. storms
5. hurricanes, typhoons
6. wind
7. the day-to-day changes in the air, measured by temperature and precipitation
8. how hot or cold the air is
9. rain, sleet, hail, or snow that falls to the ground
10. the average weather in a place over a period of many years

Section 3 Quiz

1. d   2. a   3. e   4. b   5. c
6. c   7. b   8. c   9. a   10. a

Section 4 Guided Reading

1. low latitudes
2. middle latitudes
3. high latitudes
4. rain forests
5. deciduous trees, wildflowers, grasses
6. tundra (no trees, low shrubs and grass)
7. Tropical wet: two wet seasons; tropical wet and dry: one wet and one dry season
8. There are seasonal changes, but temperatures hardly ever fall below freezing.
9. short, cold summers and long, cold winters
10. plants that grow in an area naturally
11. the uppermost branches of trees in a forest
12. cold area along the Arctic Circle that has no trees but does have low shrubs and other very small plants
13. a climate that changes in relation to the height of a mountain

Section 4 Quiz

1. e   2. a   3. d   4. b   5. c
6. c   7. b   8. b   9. d   10. a

Vocabulary Activity

1. l   2. m   3. d   4. g   5. o
6. e   7. j   8. c   9. i   10. k
11. f   12. a   13. h   14. b   15. n
16. p

Reteaching

Answers may vary. Sample answers are given.

1. Days are divided into daytime and nighttime depending on whether or not a side of the Earth is facing the sun.
2. The hours and intensity of sunlight vary at different parts of the Earth, and seasons result.
3. The continents formed.
4. Volcanoes and earthquakes result.
5. Mountains and islands build up.
6. Mountains are worn down, soil is created and deposited, and new landforms are created.
7. The region will most likely have four seasons, each lasting about three months.
8. This movement helps keep the Earth from overheating.
9. The city will be cooler in summer and warmer in winter than other places in the same latitude not near a large body of water.

Enrichment

1. They form the boundaries of the tropics. They mark the farthest distances north and south of the Equator that the sun ever shines directly overhead.
2. These lines of latitude are named after the constellations in which the sun appeared in 2 B.C. during the summer and winter solstices in the Northern Hemisphere, but the constellations in which the sun appears at those times of year have since changed.
3. either of two times of year when the sun is at its greatest distance from the Equator
4. Maps and diagrams should demonstate a clear understanding of the information in the passage.

Answer Key

Critical Thinking

1. F
2. O
3. O
4. F
5. F

Chapter 3

Section 1 Guided Reading

1. They study rates of birth, marriage, death, and reasons why people choose to live in particular areas.
2. 75 percent
3. hot deserts, dry land with little vegetation, and rugged mountains
4. major bodies of water, such as rivers and lakes
5. There were so few trees in the Great Plains that settlers had no resources to build houses.
6. Over several generations, people living in these areas learn ways of adjusting to their environments.
7. the total number of people in the world or a location
8. the way in which the population is spread out over the Earth
9. person who studies the populations of the world
10. the average number of people who live in a square mile or kilometer

Section 1 Quiz

1. F; A demographer studies the populations of the world.
2. T
3. F; Population density is the average number of people living in a square mile.
4. T
5. F; The Nile River valley has one of the highest population densities in the world.
6. b   7. c   8. c   9. a   10. d

Section 2 Guided Reading

1. Men and women usually lived less than 50 years.
2. Populations in most countries have grown very fast.
3. More babies are born healthy and people live longer than they used to.
4. Growing populations use natural resources at a faster rate than stable populations.
5. People cut trees to use the wood for building and for fuel.
6. life expectancy
7. Green Revolution
8. birthrate
9. death rate

Section 2 Quiz

1. b   2. a   3. c   4. e   5. d
6. b   7. c   8. a   9. d   10. c

Section 3 Guided Reading

1. During the 1959 revolution in Cuba, many Cubans were "pushed" to the United States. They looked for safety and for better lives.
2. Scandinavians left their country because land there was scarce. They were "pulled" to Minnesota and Wisconsin because land was free and the climate was much like their own.
3. Many Americans have moved to the southern and southwestern states in search of better climates and different jobs.
4. São Paulo is a new home for many rural South Americans seeking better housing, better jobs, and a good education for their children.
5. "push-pull" theory
6. migrates, immigrant
7. urban, rural
8. urbanization

Section 3 Quiz

1. e   2. d   3. a   4. c   5. b
6. b   7. b   8. a   9. c   10. a

Answer Key

Vocabulary Activity

Sentences will vary. Sample answers are given.

1. The population of Chicago, IL, is greater than that of Reno, NV.
2. Loren wanted to find out about the population distribution in the state of Maine.
3. The demographer noticed that the birthrate was increasing faster than the death rate in most parts of the world.
4. The population density in the Mojave Desert is quite low.
5. The discovery of modern medicines is one reason that the world's birthrate has increased.
6. The death rate is slower now than it was 200 years ago.
7. During the 1800s, the life expectancy of most men and women in the United States was about 50 years.
8. Changes in agriculture such as farming with less water and using new fertilizers to enrich the soil are called the Green Revolution.
9. During the California gold rush, there was a large migration of Chinese people to the United States.
10. Immigrants have come to the United States from all over the world.
11. The migration of South Vietnamese families supports the "push-pull" theory, because they were pushed away by their former enemies and pulled by the hope of a better life.
12. Most cities are growing quickly due to urbanization.
13. Outside the large city was a rural area consisting of farms and small villages.
14. Jakarta, Indonesia is a rapidly growing urban area.

Reteaching

1. are near an ocean, a river, or a lake; have flat land, fertile soil, and other natural resources; and have a favorable climate.
2. Asia, Europe, and North America.
3. the birthrate and the death rate.
4. increased greatly.
5. new farming methods have increased the world's food supply, and scientific advances in health and medicine treat health problems that used to kill people.
6. shortages of fresh water, energy, and food; scarcity of jobs, schools, and housing; inadequate transportation and sanitation; and damage to the environment.
7. negative things push them to leave a country, and the promise of better living conditions pulls them to another country.
8. The new government in Vietnam meant a serious change and the United States accepted the immigrants.
9. people are migrating to cities from farms and small villages.
10. not enough housing, jobs, schools, hospitals, and other services; overcrowding; noise; pollution; and traffic jams.

Enrichment

Reasons Needed

Growing world population increases the demand for food.

Wild stocks of fish are being depleted by over-fishing.

Benefits

It supplies food for the growing world population.

It helps prevent the depletion of wild stocks of fish.

Limitations and Problems

Saltwater species are harder to raise.

Concentrated fish wastes cause pollution.

Critical Thinking

1. The waters of the Colorado River are used to meet the household, irrigation, and energy needs of a large population of people in a dry region.
2. The southern part of the river is running dry, wetlands are drying up, water quality is declining, and animals at the mouth of the river are dying.

Answer Key

Chapter 4

Section 1 Guided Reading

1. advanced
2. terraces
3. hunting and gathering
4. cold
5. writing
6. the way of life of a group of people who share similar beliefs and customs
7. a particular group's individual skills, customs, and ways of doing things
8. tools and the skills to use them
9. changes to a group's environment
10. farming

Section 1 Quiz

1. F; Culture is the way of life of people who share the same beliefs and customs.
2. T
3. F; A particular group's individual skills, customs, and ways of doing things are called cultural traits.
4. T
5. T
6. a   7. b   8. c   9. c   10. d

Section 2 Guided Reading

1. Some cultures have small groups that work together to get food or protect the community.
2. Small groups such as families pass on traditions and customs of the community and of each individual family.
3. Without language, people would not be able to pass on knowledge or beliefs to future generations.
4. Languages reflect the things that are important in each culture, such as the many words for snow in the Inuit language.
5. a way of organizing people into smaller groups
6. the basic family unit in some cultures—a mother, a father, and their children

7. a family that includes several generations, such as aunts, uncles, grandparents, and cousins
8. a person's standards of correct and moral behavior

Section 2 Quiz

1. d   2. e   3. b   4. c   5. a
6. c   7. b   8. d   9. b   10. a

Section 3 Guided Reading

1. People and privately owned companies own most basic and nonbasic businesses.
2. The government owns most basic industries. Nonbasic industries are privately owned.
3. The government owns all industries. There are some private businesses, such as small farms and special stores.
4. company owners
5. the government
6. the government
7. monarchy
8. government
9. consumer
10. direct democracy
11. capitalism, socialism, communism
12. dictator
13. representative democracy

Section 3 Quiz

1. b   2. c   3. a   4. e   5. d
6. b   7. c   8. c   9. b   10. c

Section 4 Guided Reading

1. new ideas, technology such as radio and television, and changes in the environment
2. Jeans were invented in the United States but are now popular around the world.
3. The Japanese play baseball but have adapted the game to fit their own culture.
4. People do not have to wait for others to bring new ideas with them. New ideas are now sent all over the world by fax, phone, and television.

Answer Key

5. because modern transportation and commu- nication can connect faraway people, busi- nesses, and governments almost instantly

6. Most cultures recycle and make efforts to pro- tect forests and endangered species.

7. the movement of customs and ideas from one culture to another

8. the process of accepting, borrowing, and exchanging ideas among cultures

Section 4 Quiz

1. F; The movement of customs from one culture to another is called cultural diffusion.

2. F; Acculturation is the process of borrowing ideas among cultures.

3. T

4. T

5. F; If things in a culture change too fast, people can become confused and the culture is threatened.

6. b   7. c   8. a   9. d   10. b

Vocabulary Activity

1. i   2. m   3. e   4. o   5. b

6. l   7. p   8. n   9. k   10. g

11. j   12. f   13. d   14. h   15. c

16. a

Reteaching

Answers will vary. Sample answers are given.

I.

A. Culture is the way of life of a group of people who share similar beliefs and customs. Cultural traits are the individual skills, cus- toms, and ways of doing things of a particular group of people.

B. Geographers want to know how landforms, cli- mate, vegetation, and resources affect culture. They also study the effect that people have on their environment.

C. The four major stages in the development of early cultures are the invention of tools, the discovery of fire, the growth of agriculture, and the use of writing.

II.

A. Families are the basic social unit of any cul- ture, whether they are nuclear or extended, patriarchal or matriarchal.

B. Language gives people the ability to communi- cate everything they need to share in their cul- ture. It enables people to pass on their culture, and it reflects how they see their culture.

C. Religion answers questions about the purpose of life, defines important values, and provides ethics, or guidelines for behavior.

III.

A. Three basic types of economic systems are capitalism, socialism, and communism. In cap- italism, private individuals own the busi- nesses; in socialism, the government manages major industries; in communism, the govern- ment owns all basic and nonbasic industries.

B. Forms of government include monarchies, in which a king or queen rules; democracies, in which the people elect representatives who create laws; and dictatorships, in which one person has total power.

IV.

A. Cultures may change because of changes in the natural environment, technological discov- eries, or new ideas that are spread when peo- ple travel.

B. Improvements in technology have brought many benefits, but they have also caused valuable traditions to be lost.

Enrichment

1. It first spread from the Fertile Crescent to Egypt and Europe. From Egypt, it spread to Ethiopia. Then it spread from the Fertile Crescent to India and China. From Europe, it spread to Russia, North America, Central America, South America, South Africa, and Australia. Finally, it spread from Russia to Siberia.

2. from the 6000s B.C. to the A.D. 1800s, a span of 7,800 years

3. Students' estimates may vary from a few years to a few decades. A new farm product or prac- tice could spread more quickly today because

Answer Key

people around the world are connected through international communication and transportation systems.

Critical Thinking

1. Similarities: the federation of tribes was like the federation of states; both guaranteed religious and political freedom; both provided a way to impeach leaders and a way to amend laws. Difference: In the Iroquois League, women elected and removed leaders.

2. Answers will vary.

Chapter 5

Section I Guided Reading

1. renewable
2. paper, wood
3. renewable
4. food
5. recyclable
6. drinking water, soft drinks
7. nonrenewable
8. provide heat
9. any useful material found in the environment such as soil, water, minerals, and vegetation
10. a resource that must be changed before it can be used
11. a natural resource—such as water, nitrogen, or carbon—that cycles naturally through the environment
12. a resource that can be replaced, such as crops, trees, and animals raised for food
13. a resource—such as oil, coal, or natural gas—that cannot be replaced when used up
14. a nonrenewable resource—such as oil, natural gas or coal—that was created millions of years ago from the remains of prehistoric plants and animals

Section I Quiz

1. a	2. d	3. c	4. e	5. b
6. c	7. b	8. c	9. d	10. b

Section 2 Guided Reading

1. the second stage
2. people invented machines, built factories, and found new sources of power for making goods
3. wars and natural disasters
4. disease, food shortages, unsafe water, poor education and health services, and changing governments
5. commercial farming
6. foreign aid
7. subsistence farming
8. plantation
9. developing, developed
10. manufacturing

Section 2 Quiz

1. e	2. d	3. a	4. b	5. c
6. b	7. c	8. b	9. a	10. d

Section 3 Guided Reading

1. When the rain forests are gone, many plant and animal species will become extinct, or die out.
2. People have always dumped waste products into rivers, lakes, and oceans. These wastes can harm or destroy living things in the water.
3. Canada and the United States now have laws to reduce acid rain by reducing pollution.
4. Many nations agreed to get rid of ozone-destroying chemicals by the year 2000. And scientists are searching for safe chemicals to replace CFCs.
5. habitat
6. ozone layer
7. recycle
8. acid rain
9. global warming

Section 3 Quiz

1. F; A community of living things and its environment is called an ecosystem.
2. T

Answer Key

2. T

3. F; To recycle is to reuse materials to make new products.

4. F; The process of clearing land of trees is called deforestation.

5. T

6. b   7. c   8. a   9. d   10. b

Vocabulary Activity

Sentences will vary. Sample answers are given.

1. Water is an important natural resource.

2. Trees are the raw material for many products, including lumber and paper.

3. Nitrogen is an example of a recyclable resource.

4. Renewable resources include plants and other living things on the Earth.

5. Oil is an example of a nonrenewable resource.

6. Oil is a fossil fuel that is used to power cars and trucks.

7. Manufacturing creates many products, including furniture, musical instruments, computers, and bicycles.

8. Because Italy has many industries, it is considered a developed nation.

9. Many people in developing nations live in rural areas.

10. Many small, family-run farms have been replaced by commercial farming.

11. Many people in developing countries depend upon subsistence farming for food.

12. Workers on plantations usually raise one crop, such as sugar cane, coffee, cotton, or bananas.

13. Developed nations often help developing nations with foreign aid.

14. Plants and animals survive best in their natural ecosystem.

15. Many rain forests in South America are disappearing because of deforestation.

16. Old-growth redwood forests on the West Coast of the United States provide a habitat for many species of plants and animals.

17. Acid rain has caused many lakes in upstate New York to become lifeless.

18. There is strong evidence that the ozone layer is thinning over the southern parts of the Earth.

19. Global warming is also known as the greenhouse effect.

20. It is very important today to recycle as many of the things we use as possible.

Reteaching

Answers will vary. Sample answers are given.

1. trees
2. minerals
3. water
4. petroleum
5. farming
6. making plywood from trees
7. providing medical services
8. consumes great amounts of raw materials
9. food shortages
10. Plant and animal species die out.
11. Lake water becomes more acidic, and fish die.
12. fertilizers and pesticides from farms
13. burning fossil fuels
14. solar energy
15. recycling

Critical Thinking

1. Local people need income, so some illegally poach and cut timber.
2. Generate income through tourism and by employing people in conservation.
3. Local people need firewood.
4. Plant trees along field edges.
5. Local people need forest foods and medicines.
6. Allow controlled harvest of forest foods and medicinal plants.

© Prentice-Hall, Inc.

Activities and Projects

Teacher Notes

To meet the needs of middle school students, **Prentice Hall World Explorer** includes activities designed for all learning styles. Every day, you encounter students who bring a wide range of skills and abilities to the classroom. You as teacher make choices about the kinds of activities that best complement your teaching plan. This booklet is designed to make it easy for you to incorporate hands-on activities into your classroom.

With support offered in this booklet, students can work independently or in cooperative groups to perform a variety of interesting and meaningful projects. For the Activity Atlas and Activity Shops, this booklet provides recording sheets, templates for graphs or charts, and helpful background information. For the Project Possibilities described in the student text, this booklet includes a section called Book Projects that offers ideas for breaking down and organizing each task.

In addition, this booklet includes cooperative learning activities for each chapter in the unit. At least one of the cooperative activities is a simulation in which students concentrate on a real-life issue. Each cooperative activity is four pages long and includes one or two student pages, one or two teacher pages, and a rubric page. The concept and skill objectives for each cooperative learning activity are clearly stated on the teacher page supporting each activity. You can customize your assignments, using particular projects to meet the needs of specific groups of students.

At the end of this booklet are four general grading rubrics for written and oral presentations, visual displays, and models. There is also an answer key for the student pages in this booklet.

Prentice Hall World Explorer offers a wide and exciting range of options to students. Use this booklet to help you take advantage of these options.

Discovery Activities About Geography

What Kinds of Maps Does Geo Leo Need?

Directions: Use this page to complete the Geo Leo activity in your textbook Activity Atlas.

A. "If I wanted to find out how many people live in the city of Mumbai (Bombay), India, which map would I use?"

_____

_____

B. "On my trip to South Asia, I want to search for gigantic insects that live in tropical rain forests. Which map do I use to find the tropical rain forests?"

_____

_____

C. "South Asia is a region that has many different types of climate. Which map will help me bring the right gear for Pakistan's arid climate?"

_____

_____

Bonus!

• Which type of vegetation grows in only one South Asian country?

_____

_____

• Compare the vegetation and climate maps. What do you notice about the summer monsoon winds and the locations of tropical rain forests?

_____

_____

Discovery Activities About Geography

Analyze Density

Directions: Use this page to complete the population density activity in your textbook Activity Atlas. If you need help identifying the continents, refer to the World Physical map in the Atlas at the back of your textbook.

1. Which places on the population density map have many people?

_____

_____

2. Which areas have the fewest numbers of people?

_____

_____

3. Why do you think people live where they do?

_____

_____

4. What conclusions can you draw about how physical features influence where cities are located?

_____

_____

Bonus!

• What is the population density where you live? What physical features would you say influence the number of people who live in your area?

_____

_____

• If you could live anywhere, what physical features would draw you to an area? Include items such as climate, elevation, vegetation, water sources, and existing population density.

_____

_____

Discovery Activities About Geography

Create a "Mental Map"

Directions: Use this page to help with the "mental map" activity in your textbook Activity Atlas. Before you draw your map, use the chart below to record details about your destination and the route you will mark.

Your Map

Destination:
How will you get there?
Streets:
Landmarks:
Buildings:
Other points of interest:
Map details
Compass rose? (y/n)
Scale? (y/n)
Key? (y/n)
Compare your map with other maps.
How is it different?
How is it similar?

Bonus!

- Which items did you choose to include on your map? What do you notice about them?

_____

_____

Activities and Projects

The Earth's Seasons

Directions: Use this worksheet to answer questions and record results as you do the Activity Shop Lab in your textbook.

Procedure

During Step Two, the text says that something besides distance must cause the season to be winter in the United States. What do you think might be the cause?

_____

Observations

1. Which affects the seasons more—the angle at which the sun's rays hit the Earth or its distance from the sun? Explain your answer.

_____

_____

2. Which season does the Southern Hemisphere have when it is winter in the Northern Hemisphere?

_____

3. When will you have about the same amount of daylight as night—January 8, July 20, or September 22? Explain your answer.

_____

_____

Analysis and Conclusion

1. If the Earth were not tilted on its axis, how do you think the seasons would be affected? Explain your answer.

_____

_____

2. In a science fiction story, the Earth's orbit is disturbed. The planet travels in a straight line, not around the sun. How would this affect the seasons?

_____

_____

A Five-Theme Tour

Directions: Use this worksheet to plan your world tour as you do the Activity Shop Interdisciplinary in your textbook.

Decide Where You Will Go

a. River or mountain tour? _____

b. Five locations you will visit _____

Describe the Places on Your Tour

a. What is each place like? Write an exciting description of each place on a separate sheet of paper.

b. How do people use each place? How have they changed it? Add this information to your descriptions.

Plan a Travel Route

a. Destination _____

b. Starting point _____

c. Stops and total mileage _____

Learn About the Language

Use the chart to write some of the common words in the languages spoken in the places you visit.

Languages of the Region

Language	Hello	Good-bye	Thank You	Please	Other Words

BOOK PROJECT

GEOGRAPHY
TOOLS AND CONCEPTS

The Geography Game

A. Researching Geographic Information

Choose a country that you think might have interesting geographic
features, people, cultural traditions, and natural resources.

Look for information in encyclopedias, books, atlases, and magazines.
Try to choose facts that will make the country recognizable without
immediately giving it away. For example, if you describe the Grand
Canyon as a clue, most students will know right away that the country is
the United States.

Use the chart below to record facts about the country you have chosen.
Write the name of the country, and then fill in facts under each heading.
You can include more than one fact for each category. Later, you can use
the information on the chart to make the game clues.

Geography Game Clue Facts

Country:	
Physical Features	
Climate	
Population	
Cultures	
Natural Resources	

The Geography Game *(continued)*

B. Making the Clue Cards and World Map

Work in small groups to make clue cards for the game. You will need
either paper or cardboard and writing materials. Decide on a card size
that will work well and try to make all the cards that size.

Look at the information you have gathered on the Geography Game
Clue Facts chart. Decide which facts you'd like to use. When you have
decided, use scrap paper to practice writing clues. You will want your
clues to be easy to understand but at the same time not give away the
answer. Be sure you have provided enough information.

When you are happy with your clues, write them neatly on individual
cards. Then write the name of the correct country on the other side.
Shown below are sample cards with clues that describe India.

Buddhism started here.

Summer monsoons make it rain here.

Its most populous city is Mumbai (Bombay).

This country contains the Ganges River.

Cotton is one of its major exports.

BOOK PROJECT

GEOGRAPHY
TOOLS AND CONCEPTS

The Geography Game *(continued)*

C. Play the Game

Now that you have finished the cards, you can play the game. When it is your team's turn, you will work together to guess a country. Since you will have 30 seconds to answer, you might try giving each person a chance to make a suggestion. Then you can use the suggestions to arrive at the answer for your group. If you don't agree on a single answer, take a quick vote. Use the tally sheet below to keep track of the score.

Score Card

Team 1	
Team 2	
Team 3	

World News Today

A. Collecting and Organizing Articles

Where will you find news articles about natural resources and economies around the world? Newspapers and newsmagazines often have articles about the economies of different countries or regions of the world. They may have articles about natural resources as well. Other sources of information include library books, encyclopedias, and almanacs. If you have access to the Internet or other on-line services, you may find sources of information through your computer.

Use the chart below to keep a record of useful articles. Then briefly summarize important ideas from the articles. Use additional sheets of paper as needed. Remember that you will be choosing a single country and learning about the relationship between its economy and natural resources.

Article Organizer

Title and Source of Article	Country or Region	Natural Resources	Economy and Business

BOOK PROJECT

GEOGRAPHY
TOOLS AND CONCEPTS

World News Today *(continued)*

B. Making and Displaying the Poster

You can use the newspaper and magazine clippings that you have gathered to make a poster. Begin by choosing one country to feature on your poster. Cut out or photocopy interesting news articles and decide how you want them to appear on the poster.

Use the table below to write a final bibliography for your poster. You can cut out the table and post it next to your competed poster.

Bibliography of Sources

Title	Author	Source	Date/Volume	Page Numbers

When your poster is finished, display it in the classroom. Look at other posters and compare the articles you find. Discuss with other students the different topics, pointing out similarities and differences among countries and regions of the world.

World News Today *(continued)*

C. Prepare and Give a Talk About Natural Resources and Economies

Prepare a talk about your poster and the information you found. Look at the notes you took as you prepared the poster. Note the important points you wrote there. Reread the articles and take notes. You can use these notes to prepare your speech.

As you gather information, be sure to focus on the relationship between natural resources and economy and business. You will want to be able to clearly explain this relationship as you speak. Note how different natural resources are used and who uses them. Point out ways in which natural resources benefit the people and businesses of a country.

The checklist below can help you remember some of the basic techniques for giving a good talk. It is divided into two parts: one that covers the content of your speech and the other that has suggestions for giving a good speech.

Checklist for Your Talk

Important Points to Remember	
Natural Resources	
Economy and Business	

Giving a Good Speech	
Loud Enough	Everyone should be able to hear you.
Clear Voice	All words should be easy to understand.
Audience Contact	Look at the audience as well as your notes.
Relaxed Manner	Speak slowly and take deep breaths if you're nervous.

Activities and Projects

GEOGRAPHY
TOOLS AND CONCEPTS

Focus on Part of the Whole

A. The Amazing World Around Us

Which region or country of the world will you choose for this project?
You might begin by thinking about places or people in the world that you
find particularly interesting. Ask yourself: What regions would I most
like to learn about? If you are having trouble, look at a world map or
an atlas for ideas. You might decide to choose an area that is above
10,000 feet (3,048 m) in elevation. Or you might like to learn more about
life on a South Pacific island. Think of climates or physical features that
might have a strong influence on how people live. Find several good
examples from which to choose. As you begin your research, use the
chart below to keep a record of important facts and information about
each region. This will help you make a final decision.

World Regions

Region	Physical Characteristics	Effects on People	Additional Information

Choose the region that you think would be the most fun to learn more about.

Focus on Part of the Whole
(continued)

GEOGRAPHY
TOOLS AND CONCEPTS

B. Researching and Organizing Information

Where is the best place to look for information about regions of the world and the people who live there? You can begin by going to your school or local library. Ask the librarian in either place for help. You will probably find useful information in encyclopedias. Magazines, such as *National Geographic,* can have very helpful articles. Atlases, almanacs, and books on a specific region will also have useful facts for your display.

You can photocopy or write summaries of information that you find.

Use the table below to keep a record of where you found useful and interesting information.

Sources of Information

Title of Article	Subject	Source of Article

BOOK PROJECT

Focus on Part of the Whole
(continued)

C. Making a Display
Here are some suggestions for making your display.

Materials
photocopy of a map of your region
overhead projector (if available)
large sheets of paper
colored markers and pencils
paints
crayons
glue
scissors

Procedure
1. If you have access to an overhead projector, have your teacher help you project a map outline of the region or country you have chosen. Then trace it onto a large sheet of paper. If you do not have an overhead projector, copy the map outline by hand.

2. When you have copied the map outline, include important physical features, such as bodies of water, mountains, elevations, and deserts. You can use paints, markers, crayons, or other art materials to do this. If you are working with a group, divide up the jobs. Work in pairs or threes, so that you will not get in each other's way.

3. Write your captions on separate sheets of paper. Be sure they are neat and easy to read. When they are just the way you want them, cut them out and glue them in place on your map. Your captions should explain how the land and climate have affected the people in the region and how the people have affected the land. If you have photographs of the land or people, you might include them on the map next to the captions.

4. Look at your display and notice anything that you might have left out. Have you shown clearly how the geography and climate have affected people's lives? Are there any parts that are confusing? When your display is finished, share it with the class.

Desktop Countries

A. Conducting an Interview

When you have chosen a country for your project, think of someone
who might have lived there. Or think of someone who might have
friends or relatives who know about the country, its land, and its people.
You may have to ask several people before you find the right person to
interview. You could also interview more than one person.

When you interview someone, there are some important things to
remember. First you must prepare for the interview by learning as much
as you can about the topic. Then write down the questions you want to
ask. What do you want to learn? Try to avoid questions that can be
answered with yes or no. For example, you might ask an immigrant to
compare daily life in his or her home country with life in the United
States.

When you conduct the interview, be very polite and respectful. Ask for
permission to use a tape recorder. This is the best way to remember all
the details of what is said. Try to make the person feel that his or her
story is important. You can make a bigger version of the chart below to
prepare for your interview and record what you have learned.

Preparing and Conducting an Interview

Questions	Responses

Use the information you have gathered to help prepare your "desktop country."

Desktop Countries *(continued)*

B. Preparing a Recipe

If you know someone from the country you have chosen, ask him or her to describe a favorite dish. You might suggest that the dish be fairly easy to make, but you can decide this for yourself. You might also be able to find a cookbook with dishes from the country.

Remember that you will prepare the dish at home and then bring it to school. Talk to your teacher about what dishes would work. Should your dish be served hot? If so, is there a way to heat up food at your school? Who will provide plates and utensils? You might ask an adult family member to help you with this part of the project.

Once you have chosen a recipe, talk to your family about when you can prepare it. Ask for help if you need it. You might also want to work with a friend. Write the ingredients for the recipe in the space below.

_____   _____

_____   _____

_____   _____

_____   _____

_____   _____

_____   _____

Check that you have all the ingredients you need before you begin. Be sure to follow the recipe carefully. Most recipes are not hard to prepare if you work step-by-step. Whenever you cook, use hot pads to avoid burns.

When you bring your dish to share with the class, be sure to let everyone know all of the ingredients. Some students may have food allergies and should be aware of what they are eating.

If possible, tell students how the dish you have prepared is part of the culture of your "desktop country." Are the ingredients commonly found there? Is the dish used for particular special occasions?

Desktop Countries *(continued)*

C. Make a Desktop Display

To make your desktop display, you will want to organize your research information, interview notes, and drawings. Remember, you don't need a lot of information or many objects. Choose what will say something important about the country.

Materials

paper
paints, markers, colored pencils, crayons
scissors
glue
tape
souvenir items from the country
craft sticks

Procedure

1. Begin by reviewing your research. Choose facts and information that you think other students would like to know about your country. You might tell about unusual land formations, products for which the country is best known, or important traditions, art, or music.

2. Use photographs and writing to illustrate the information you have chosen to include. Remember, your entire display must fit on your desktop. If you have souvenir items, choose those you want to display. Then write a card to explain each item.

3. Make a country flag. If you don't know the flag of the country, look it up in an encyclopedia or atlas. Use craft sticks to make a pole, and fly your flag from your desk!

4. If possible, include a map of the country that shows major cities, landforms, and other important features.

5. Carefully label each item. You will want other students to look at your desktop and be able to learn about your country.

COOPERATIVE LEARNING ACTIVITY

CHAPTER 1

The World of Geography

Plotting a Route Around the World

In this activity, your team will plan a trip around the world. Your route should include 10 stopping points. Your stopping points can be anywhere you would like to stay—from the largest cities to the most remote islands, mountaintops, or rain forests. When you have plotted your route, you will mark it on a map. Then you will trade latitude and longitude information with another team and mark each other's routes on your maps.

Background

Every location on the Earth can be found by knowing its longitude and latitude. These are imaginary lines that divide the globe vertically and horizontally. Latitude lines are parallel to the Equator. They are measured from 0° at the Equator to 90°N at the North Pole and 90°S at the South Pole. When you write latitudes, the lines above the Equator are followed by N, which stands for the word *north.* All lines south of the Equator are followed by S, which stands for the word *south.* Longitude lines are numbered from 0° to 180°. The Prime Meridian, or 0°, is the one that passes through Greenwich, England. Longitude lines are followed by an E or a W, for *east* or *west,* depending upon their location. There is only one longitude line at 180°. It is exactly opposite 0° and is called the International Date Line.

Procedure

1. **Make your map.** Read all the steps in this project. Then meet with your group to divide the jobs. Begin by working with your team to mark the latitude and longitude lines on a blank map of the world. Label each line with its number and correct letter: N for *north,* S for *south,* E for *east,* and W for *west.* You will have to find the correct scale for the size of your map.

2. Choose stopping places. Choose the 10 stopping places for your route. Write each one in the table below, along with its latitude and longitude. Mark these locations on the map. Label each location with its latitude and longitude. Connect the points with a colored line. The line should go completely around the world.

Stopping Places Around the World

Stopping Place	Latitude	Longitude

3. Trade stopping places. Give the list in the table above to another team. When you have traded, use the other team's list to plot their route on your map. Mark this route with a different color. Label each point with its latitude and longitude.

4. Find out more about your route. Work with a partner and choose one or two points on your team's route. These might be major cities, landforms, or bodies of water. Then find out more about the locations you have chosen. Write a brief report that includes interesting information about the land, climate, people, history, or culture for each location. If possible, try to find photographs. Use what you have learned to add drawings or other decorations to your map.

Activities and Projects

The World of Geography

Plotting a Route Around the World

Content Objectives
- Students will gain a deeper understanding of latitude and longitude.
- Students will learn about cities, landforms, and bodies of water around the world.

Skill Objectives
- Using Route Maps
- Locating Information
- Writing for a Purpose—Report

Advance Preparation
You will need to find and photocopy a world map for students that does not contain latitude and longitude lines. It does not matter whether or not the map contains country borders.

Suggested group size: six students

Suggested time: 60 minutes for marking latitude and longitude lines; 60 minutes for choosing and marking routes; 40 minutes for marking another team's route; 20 minutes for discussion

Procedure
Divide the class into teams. Distribute student pages and have students start planning their projects. You may wish to distribute a copy of the rubric for maps to each team.

Students may need help working out the scale for marking latitude and longitude lines. Explain that they simply need to divide the total number of degrees by the number of inches on the map (horizontally for longitude and vertically for latitude). For example, there are 90° from the Equator to the North Pole. If there are 6 inches between the Equator and the pole, the scale will be 1 inch = 15°.

After students have completed their maps, have them share the maps with the class. Group members can talk about important features along the route. You might encourage other students to ask questions about the stopping places on the routes.

The World of Geography

Maps will be evaluated according to the following rubric.

Rubric for Maps

	Awesome	Admirable	Acceptable
Research	Students find five or six interesting facts about all the points along their route.	Students find three or four interesting facts about all the points along their route.	Students find one or two facts about a few points along their route.
Accuracy	Students draw latitude and longitude lines very accurately. Each location is exactly where it should be and marked with the correct latitude and longitude.	Students draw latitude and longitude lines accurately. Each location is well marked and in the correct place.	Students draw latitude and longitude lines fairly accurately. Most of the locations are in the correct places and well marked.
Presentation	Maps are neatly and clearly drawn. All points and lines are easy to find and follow. Students decorate their maps beautifully with colors, drawings, or photos.	Maps are neatly and clearly drawn. All points and lines are easy to find.	Maps are drawn well. Most of the points and lines are easy to find.
Teamwork	All team members contribute equally to the project. They help one another and give constructive feedback.	Students work well as a team.	Team members may work well together, but some students do more work than others.

Activities and Projects

CHAPTER
2

Earth's Physical Geography

Simulation: Making a Poster for The Whitney Classic

You have been asked to create a poster for a bicycle race in California. The race sponsor would like you to use a contour line that represents the changes in elevation between the start and finish of the race. Along the contour line, you will include several scenes that show the vegetation at different elevations. To prepare for this assignment, you will work with a group to find out about the vegetation and climate changes that take place as you travel from Death Valley to Mount Whitney.

Background

The Whitney Classic is a bicycle race in California from Death Valley National Park to Mount Whitney. It begins at Badwater, 282 feet (86 m) below sea level. This is the lowest point in the United States. In two days, racers ride 136 miles (219 km) to the end of Whitney Portal Road, at around 8,000 feet (2,591 m). This spot is as high as you can drive up the mountain, which at around 14,495 feet (4,418 m) is the highest peak in the United States outside of Alaska.

Between Death Valley National Park and Mount Whitney, the racers must climb the Panamint Mountains, descend into the Panamint Valley, then climb the Inyo Mountains and drop down into the Owens Valley. After crossing the Owens Valley, they begin the actual climb of Mount Whitney. The Owens Valley is under 4,000 feet (1,219 m) in elevation. When you look up at Mount Whitney from the valley, it stands more than 10,000 feet (3,048 m) above you.

Procedure

1. **Find elevations.** Read all the steps of this project. Then meet with your group to divide the jobs. Find Death Valley and Mount Whitney on a physical map of California. Note how the land rises and falls between the two areas. Assign two members to find elevations for the following places:
    *   the lowest point in Death Valley
    *   a high peak in the Panamint Mountains
    *   Panamint Springs, CA
    *   a high peak in the Inyo Range
    *   Lone Pine, CA
    *   Whitney Portal

2. **Develop a scale.** Develop a scale for your drawing. Remember that this is an art project. Your drawing does not have to be exact in scale. In order to make the image look strong, you will probably have to use two scales: one for the distance over land and one for elevation. Try 1 inch = 3 miles for the distance. This will make the length of the drawing about 3 feet. Then use 1 inch = 2,000 feet for the elevations, which will make the peak of Mount Whitney a little over 7 inches tall.

3. **Draw the contour line.** Use a pencil to draw a line along the bottom of a sheet of paper. Once you have determined the scale, calculate the distance between Mount Whitney and Badwater. Mark these two points along the line. Then find the distances between each of your elevation points. Use the distance scale to mark them on the paper. Then, using the elevation scale, mark an elevation point above the line for each location. Connect the points with lines. This will give you a general idea of the contours of the landscape. The more points you use, the more accurate your contour line will be.

4. **Add illustrations.** When you have drawn the elevation contours on the poster, research information about plant and animal life for different locations. Find out how the vegetation changes for every 1 inch, or 2,000 feet, in elevation. When you have found information, attach drawings or photos to the poster that show what the landscape looks like.

5. **Finish the poster.** Finally, write a title for your poster and information such as date and time. The race is usually held in late September.

Activities and Projects

Earth's Physical Geography

Simulation: Making a Poster for The Whitney Classic

Objectives
- Students will use research and art to learn about the land contours between the lowest and highest points in the United States outside Alaska.
- Students will gain a greater understanding of how elevation affects plant and animal life.

Skill Objectives
- Interpreting Diagrams and Illustrations
- Locating Information
- Organizing Information

Advance Preparation
Gather the following materials:
- large sheets of paper
- tape, glue
- markers, crayons, paints
- maps

You will probably need to gather reference sources about elevations and vegetation for the areas in this project. The United States Geologic Service publishes two topographic maps that cover the area from Death Valley to Mount Whitney. They are named "Fresno" and "Death Valley." These can be ordered through most camping stores. As an alternative, you can use a good road map, which will give enough elevations to draw a basic contour line.

Suggested group size: six students

Suggested time: 60 minutes for cutting out the poster shape, finding elevation points, and marking them on the poster; 40 minutes for researching information about vegetation; 40 minutes for illustrating the poster

Procedure
Divide the class into teams. Distribute student pages and have students start planning their projects. You may wish to distribute a copy of the rubric for posters to each team.

You might suggest to students that they divide the work on this project. Jobs for different team members might include
- finding elevations for points along the race,
- drawing the contour line on the poster,
- researching and drawing information about plant and animal life to illustrate the poster.

Earth's Physical Geography

Posters will be evaluated according to the following rubric.

Rubric for Posters

	Awesome	Admirable	Acceptable
Research	Students find interesting information about plants and animals for several different elevations along the racecourse.	Students find information about plants and animals for four or five different elevations along the racecourse.	Students find one or two facts about a few elevations along the racecourse.
Accuracy	The elevation contour is very accurate. Students use many points along the racecourse to create a detailed representation of the elevation.	The elevation contour is accurate. Students use some points along the racecourse to show the basic elevations.	The elevation contour is fairly accurate. Students use just a few points to show the elevations along the racecourse.
Presentation	Posters are neat and beautiful to look at. Students include attractive drawings or photos of the different animals and plants along the racecourse.	Posters are neatly made and include drawings or photos of plants and animals along the racecourse.	Posters are neatly made and include one or two scenes from different elevations along the racecourse.
Teamwork	All team members contribute equally to the project. They help one another and give constructive feedback.	Students work well as a team. They divide up the work of researching, contour-drawing, and illustrating.	Team members may work well together, but some students do more work than others.

Activities and Projects

COOPERATIVE LEARNING ACTIVITY

Earth's Human Geography

Making an Immigration Map

In this activity, you will choose one group of people and learn about when and where they migrated. The people could be your ancestors or any group that you find interesting. Then you will make a map that identifies them and shows where they moved. If you like, you can include information about how many moved, when they moved, and how many returned home.

Background

The very first people to settle in North and South America migrated from Asia across the Bering Strait to what is today Alaska. They moved slowly south through what is now Canada, the United States, and Mexico, and eventually into Central and South America.

Throughout history, people have moved from place to place. Some groups settled in specific locations, while others looked for new climates, food sources, and lands. People have traveled over land and water and, more recently, in the air. They are moving constantly. Many people have come to the United States. The United States is made up of people from all over the world. Many people have moved to other countries. For example, there are Chinese communities in Canada, Mexico, and parts of Central and South America. Many Turkish people have moved to Germany, and Algerians have moved to France.

1. **Research a group of immigrants.** Read all the steps in this project. Then meet with your group and divide up the jobs. Choose the people whose migration you wish to track. Then use encyclopedias, almanacs, or other library reference books to find out where and when these people migrated. Also find out why they migrated. Write stories about the journeys and any other interesting information you can find.

2. **Make a map.** Create a large map of the world for all the groups in the class to use. This might be done with an overhead projector, or you can copy a world map on a large scale. When the map is finished, put it on a wall or bulletin board.

3. **Mark routes.** After your group has gathered the information you need, mark your route of migration on the small map below. Then, use this map as a guide to carefully mark your route on the large classroom map. Label it neatly and clearly, giving as much information as you can. You might include the dates of the migration and the number of people who migrated. Be sure to leave room for other routes that might be in the same area.

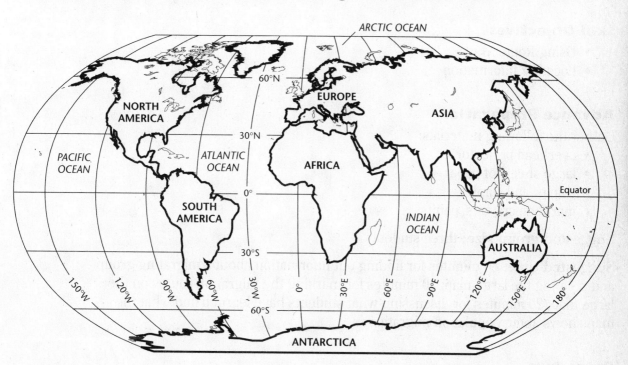

4. **Display your map.** When your map is done, display it in the classroom for other teams to observe.

CHAPTER
3

Earth's Human Geography

Making an Immigration Map

Content Objectives
- Students will gain a deeper understanding of population migrations.
- Students will learn more about particular people who have moved from one place to another.

Skill Objectives
- Using Route Maps
- Locating Information

Advance Preparation
Gather the following materials:
- overhead projector
- large sheets of paper
- stapler and staples
- markers, crayons, paints

Suggested group size: three students

Suggested time: 80 minutes for finding out information about a migrating group and creating the large map; 20 minutes for marking the migration routes on the large map; 20 minutes for discussing what students have learned and what the map shows about population migrations

Procedure

Divide the class into teams. Distribute students' pages and have students begin to work on the project. You may wish to give a copy of the rubric for maps to each group. Either choose students to make the one large map as other students research their routes, or prepare a large map for the class to use beforehand.

Before students begin to mark the large map, find out whether many of the routes will overlap. If so, have students work carefully to be sure there is room for each group's arrows. When students are marking on the large map, suggest that they begin with pencil. When they are sure the route is correct, they can use markers or crayons.

When the large map is finished, have a class discussion. If students have specific information about the groups they have chosen, have them share it with the class. This might include stories about why people moved, how they traveled, and how their lives changed once they settled in a new place.

Earth's Human Geography

Maps will be evaluated according to the following rubric.

Rubric for Maps

	Awesome	Admirable	Acceptable
Research	Students find many interesting stories about the migration of the group they studied. They provide interesting personal accounts of people's travels.	Students find a lot of information about the group they studied, including one or two personal accounts of the migration.	Students find enough information about the group they studied. They find out why they moved and what the move was like.
Accuracy	Maps are carefully drawn and very accurate. Each route is clearly marked and includes correct dates and other information.	Maps are accurate. The routes are easy to find and follow.	Maps are fairly accurate. Most of the information is correct, and the routes are easy to find.
Presentation	Map routes are clear and easy to understand. They are well drawn and include extra information and illustrations.	Map routes are neatly marked and labeled. They include important information about the migration.	Maps are fairly clear. Most of the information is easy to read and understand.
Teamwork	All team members contribute equally to the project. They help one another and give constructive feedback.	Students work well as a team.	Team members may work well together, but some students do more work than others.

Activities and Projects

COOPERATIVE LEARNING ACTIVITY

Cultures of the World

Creating a Report on World Music

In this activity, you will work with a group to discover music from different cultures. You will choose a culture or people from another part of the world. Then you will find sound recordings and information about their lives, their music, and where they live. Your group will present what it has learned to the rest of the class.

Background

During the past 50 years, many people have said that the world has "grown smaller." You know that the distances around the world are the same as they have always been. However, we can now communicate more quickly and easily than ever before. Radio and television signals are beamed to all parts of the planet. People in remote areas such as the Himalaya Mountains and South Pacific islands watch American television shows and listen to pop music. You can hear music from almost all world cultures on many radio stations. Recordings of music from other countries are available in many record stores.

Musicians and songwriters worldwide are hearing one another's music. Master Indian musician Ravi Shankar tells how excited he was when he first heard European classical music. As a young music student, he had never heard a western orchestra. Today, this type of event happens all the time. Each day, cultures mix through their music. For example, American pop musicians like Paul Simon and David Byrne have used African and Brazilian music in their songs. The band "Los Lobos" mixes traditional Mexican songs with rock and roll. These days, it is possible to hear music from other parts of the world and not even realize it.

Procedure

1. **Choose a country.** Read all the steps in this project. Then meet with your group and divide up the jobs. Work with your group to choose a country or culture that interests you. Or, you might use a globe and pick a spot that none of you knows much about. Then use your library, local music stores, music teachers, and other adults to find out about the music, instruments, lands, and people of this place.

2. **Research a culture.** Begin your research by finding out about the people and culture of the place you have chosen. What are their lives like? What is their history? What foods do they eat? What kinds of work do they do? What types of entertainment are popular? Write a brief report that you can use to accompany recordings of their music. Try to include photographs of some of the people and their land.

3. **Research the music.** Find sound recordings from the culture. As a group, choose two or three favorite recordings that you wish to share with the class. Include in your report any information you find about the instruments and music.

4. **Prepare a presentation.** Prepare a presentation of what you have learned. Each group member should be able to give a short talk about some aspect of the people and their music. Be able to show other students where the culture can be found on a world map or globe.

5. **Present the music.** Share what you have learned with the class. Play the recordings for the class and give your short presentation about the culture. You might ask students the following questions (be prepared to answer them as you lead the discussion).
   • Can you identify the instruments?
   • Does any of the music sound familiar?
   • If so, where have you heard it before?

Activities and Projects

CHAPTER 4

Cultures of the World

Creating a Report on World Music

Content Objectives
- Students will deepen their understanding of cultures from around the world.
- Students will learn how music affects world culture.

Skill Objectives
- Drawing Conclusions
- Writing for a Purpose—Report
- Locating and Organizing Information

Advance Preparation
You will need a phonograph, CD player, and tape player.

Suggested group size: four students

Suggested time: 80 minutes for researching information and sound recordings (you may want to allow extra time outside of class); 80 minutes for preparing reports; 40 minutes for presenting reports

Procedure
Divide the class into teams. Distribute student pages and have students start planning their projects. You may wish to distribute a copy of the rubric for reports to each team.

Encourage students to find a culture that is quite different from that of anyone in the group. As students choose a culture, help them find information and recordings. If they are having trouble, look for public radio shows that play music from other parts of the world. The programmers may know of resources that students can use. Some recordings of world music contain detailed notes and may provide useful information.

After students present their recordings, you might encourage a class discussion about the music. As the presentations are given, you might ask students to look for similarities in music from different cultures.

Cultures of the World

Reports will be evaluated according to the following rubric.

Rubric for Reports

	Awesome	Admirable	Acceptable
Research	Students find many sound recordings and a great deal of information. Their reports may contain personal profiles of one or two people from the culture.	Students find good examples of the music and interesting facts about the people and how they live.	Students will find one or two musical examples and enough information about the culture.
Writing	Reports are well organized and support the recorded material in a clear and logical way. Students include many fascinating facts about the culture and its music.	Reports are well written and provide a strong background for the music that is played.	Reports are clear and easy to understand. Students include information about the culture and its music.
Presentation	When students speak, they engage their audience, use a lively tone, and show a strong knowledge of the subject.	Students capture the attention of their audience. They speak clearly and are easy to understand.	Students keep the attention of their audience, and speak clearly for most of the presentation.
Teamwork	All team members contribute equally to the project. They help one another research, write, and prepare the report.	Students work well as a team. Each member makes an important contribution to the presentation.	Team members may work well together, but some students do more work than others.

Activities and Projects

COOPERATIVE LEARNING ACTIVITY

Earth's Natural Resources

Community Service Project—Protect the Environment

When you read about pollution in the world you might say, "How can I do anything to stop this?" Water, air, soil, even the upper atmosphere are affected. Some wild animals are endangered. Many people feel helpless about pollution. They are convinced that there's nothing they can do to make changes. However, the best cure for this helpless feeling is to act. A good way to start is with a small local project. You and your class will discover that you can make a difference. Answer these questions about your community.

- Do you live near a lake, a stream, a river, or an ocean? How clean are the beaches? Could you organize a clean-up program?
- Are paper, plastic, glass, and metal easy to recycle? What could you do to improve recycling efforts in your community?
- Do you, your family, your friends, and your neighbors conserve resources? How could you help people learn how to use less?
- Does your family use pesticides or other poisons? Do you know how these materials affect the environment and how they can become part of the water system? What can you learn about alternatives to let other people know about the dangers of using poisons?
- Do you know people who use hazardous materials? Do they dispose of them in a safe way? What can you do to educate people about using and disposing of hazardous materials? Where can you find information?
- Are there good routes for walking and bike riding where you live? Could there be safer bike paths and bike lanes? How could you organize people to encourage your local government to provide alternatives to driving?
- Do you use a lot of paper? How could you use less? What do you know about using recycled paper? Are you aware that some recycled paper uses more trees than others? How can you let other people know about different types of paper and ways to use less?

1. **Brainstorm.** Read all the steps in this project. Then answer the questions about the environment as a group. Brainstorm other ideas for projects that could be done in your community. Which are the projects that your group would like to be involved in? Write some ideas below.

_____

_____

_____

_____

_____

_____

_____

_____

_____

_____

_____

2. **Choose a project.** Work with your group to choose the project you like best. After you have chosen, take some time to outline what jobs need to be done. These could include research, writing, publishing an educational fact sheet, and talking to community members or groups. Or, you might plan a clean-up day for a park or beach. When you have divided up the jobs, begin work. Be sure you have at least two people who will keep track of
   • who is doing each job,
   • when jobs need to be done,
   • whether or not jobs have been completed.

3. **Carry out your plan.** Some jobs may need to be done outside of the classroom. Be sure that you organize your time well. Give each other and your families plenty of advance notice. After you have completed your project, meet as a class to discuss
   • what you have accomplished,
   • how you can continue or expand your project,
   • how you think you have affected your community,
   • other community service projects that you might like to do.

CHAPTER
5

Earth's Natural Resources

Community Service Project—Protect the Environment

Content Objectives
- Students will work together to plan, prepare, and complete a community service project.
- Students will learn how to work as a group and try to educate others about protecting the environment.

Skill Objectives
Objectives will depend upon the specific project that students choose. The following are possible:
- Expressing Problems Clearly
- Identifying Central Issues
- Recognizing Bias
- Reading Tables and Analyzing Statistics
- Recognizing Cause and Effect
- Locating Information
- Organizing Your Time

Advance Preparation
Preparation will vary according to the projects.

Suggested group size: whole class or groups of 6 to 8

Suggested time: 40 minutes for class discussion and choosing a project; 40 minutes for organizing jobs and beginning work; 80 minutes for completing the project and for discussion. (Some projects, such as a beach cleanup, will require time outside of class.)

Procedure
Divide the class into teams. Distribute student pages and have students start planning their projects. You may wish to distribute a copy of the rubric for projects to each team.

For this project, you can divide the class into two or three groups. Have each group choose a project they would like to do. Or, you might have the entire class work together on a single project.

Students will need to schedule time outside of class to work on their project. You may wish to let parents know about what students are doing and, if necessary, send home permission slips.

Earth's Natural Resources

Projects will be evaluated according to the following rubric.

Rubric for Projects

	Awesome	Admirable	Acceptable
Research	Students will find a large amount of information, which they can use to educate others.	Students find several facts that help them communicate their message.	Students find some facts to make their case for protecting the environment.
Planning/ Organization	Students are very well organized. They plan their time so that each job is carried out efficiently and the project is completed smoothly.	Students are well organized and plan their time carefully.	Students plan their time fairly well and are mostly clear about who is responsible for each part of the project.
Effectiveness	Projects have a strong impact on the community. They educate people in the community, and students receive positive feedback from many sources.	Projects communicate a clear, strong message to the community about protecting the environment.	Projects make a clear statement about the need to clean up and protect the environment.
Teamwork	Students work together as an effective team to plan, coordinate, and complete their project. Each group member plays a significant part in the work.	Students work well together and help one another complete different aspects of the project.	Students work with each other fairly well. Some students may do more work on the project than others.

Activities and Projects

Assessment of a Written Presentation

Use this rubric to assess students' essays, written reports, and any other written materials such as captions for maps or diagrams.

	Awesome	Admirable	Acceptable	Unacceptable
Creativity	The presentation has a highly interesting topic that is conveyed in an extremely engaging manner. Students include several original ideas, including some that are unusual.	The presentation has an interesting topic that is conveyed in an engaging manner. Students include one or two original ideas.	The presentation has an appropriate topic that is conveyed with a few interesting details.	The topic of the presentation may be inappropriate, and/or students use only obvious examples to back up their main points.
Content	The presentation includes excellent information gathered from a variety of sources. All the elements, such as captions for illustrations and the title, are concise and informative.	The presentation includes good information gathered from three or four sources. The project's general conclusions are supported by the data presented.	The information in the presentation is relevant, but students may have used only two reference sources.	The information in the presentation may not be relevant to the topic, and/or students use only one reference source, resulting in a limited understanding of the subject.
Organization	The information is very well organized and conveyed in a logical order. Each main point is supported by interesting and appropriate details.	The information is conveyed in a logical order, and the report is easy to follow and understand.	The information is presented in a logical order, and the supporting details almost always follow the appropriate main points.	The information is not presented logically, and supporting details are either missing or misplaced.
Spelling, Grammar, and Neatness	The written material is very neat and attractively presented. Students use correct spelling and grammar.	The written material is attractive and neat. Students make very few spelling or grammatical errors.	The written material is legible. Students make a few spelling and grammatical errors.	The written material is mostly legible, but some sections are very hard to read. Students make several spelling and grammatical errors.

Assessment of an Oral Presentation

Use this rubric to assess students' oral reports and their public speaking skills.

	Awesome	Admirable	Acceptable	Unacceptable
Content	The presentation is highly persuasive and informative. Students emphasize important information about the topic and include many fascinating details in their presentation.	The presentation is persuasive and informative. Students include pertinent information about the topic and illustrate their points with three or four interesting details.	The presentation is informative. Students convey correct information about the topic and illustrate their points with one or two details.	The presentation is somewhat or not at all informative. Some of the information in it may be incorrect. Students make only broad statements about the topic, giving few or no details.
Preparation	Students gather information from several appropriate sources. They prepare note cards to guide them as they speak and create attractive visual aids to enhance the presentation.	Students gather information from three or four sources. They prepare notes to use while they speak and create informative visual aids for the presentation.	Students gather information from one or two sources. Instead of preparing notes, they write the report word-for-word as it will be given.	Students use only one reference source to prepare for the presentation. They may be unable to complete their presentation because of lack of preparation.
Organization	The information is very well organized, logically ordered, and easy to follow. Students include interesting and appropriate examples to support their main points.	Students convey the information in a logical order, and the presentation is easy to follow and understand.	Students present the information in a logical order. Generally, the supporting details follow the main points.	The information is not presented logically, and supporting details are either missing or misplaced.
Speaking	Students are enthusiastic during the presentation. They enunciate clearly, project well, maintain eye contact with their audience, and speak in complete sentences.	Students are engaged during the presentation. They enunciate clearly, project well, and speak mostly in complete sentences.	Students present their material clearly and try to maintain eye contact.	Students come across as disinterested during the presentation. They may be hard to understand and speak in fragmented sentences.

Activities and Projects

Assessment of a Visual Display

Use this rubric to assess students' maps, diagrams, murals, graphs, illustrated stories or articles, and any other visual displays.

	Awesome	Admirable	Acceptable	Unacceptable
Content	The display conveys accurate information from several appropriate sources. Students include excellent renditions of all the necessary elements, such as a title and a legend for a map.	The display conveys accurate information from more than one source. Students include all the necessary elements, such as clearly labeled axes on a graph.	The display conveys accurate information from a reliable source. Important elements are present and convey most of the necessary information.	The display may contain inaccurate information. Important elements, such as the legend for a map, are missing.
Creativity	Students employ a highly innovative approach to creating the display. They combine several original ideas with existing materials to create a unique display.	Students combine one or two original ideas with existing materials to create an interesting display.	Students create an informative display that includes a few interesting ideas or details.	Rather than using their own ideas to make a unique display, students copy from an existing source.
Color and Form	Elements of the display are highly attractive and compatible with other elements. Whenever possible, students use colors to convey information instead of as mere decoration.	Elements of the display are attractive and work well together. Students use colors that are appropriate to the subject matter and often convey content as well as being decorative.	Elements of the display are the correct size and in the correct places. Students pay sufficient attention to conveying content with color.	Some elements of the display may be inappropriately sized. For example, a map legend may be larger than the map itself. Colors are used haphazardly.
Drawing and Labeling	Students are very careful and neat when they render their display; for example, they use straightedges to draw lines. All necessary parts of diagrams and maps are labeled clearly.	Students carefully draw elements of their displays so that the information in them is easy to understand. They include appropriate labels whenever necessary.	Students create a generally neat and readable display. They include some good labels, most of which are easy to read.	Several elements in the display are hurriedly drawn and sloppy. Students use too few labels, or the labels do not convey the correct information.

Assessment of a Model

Use this rubric to assess students' models, dioramas, and any other three-dimensional projects.

	Awesome	Admirable	Acceptable	Unacceptable
Research	Students conduct extensive research for their model, using several appropriate sources. They gather more material than they eventually use, resulting in a high level of precision.	Students gather information from three or four appropriate and varied sources. For example, they use the Internet or magazines as well as general encyclopedias.	Students gather information from one or two appropriate sources. They may rely very heavily on only one of the sources.	Students use only one reference source to prepare their model, resulting in a limited understanding of the subject.
Content	The model is an excellent representation of the scene or phenomenon being studied. Students exhibit a thorough understanding of how the model relates to the real world.	Students use the model to accurately depict a particular scene or phenomenon. Students can explain how the model works and answer questions about their work.	Students create a model that demonstrates a particular scene or phenomenon. They mostly understand how their model relates to the real world.	The model shows a scene or demonstrates a phenomenon, but it contains errors or incongruous elements, such as a human and a dinosaur in the same scene.
Quality of Construction	The model is very sturdy and well constructed. In dioramas, glue, tape, and other such materials are hidden, resulting in a highly realistic scene.	The model is sturdy. In dioramas, construction materials such as glue and tape are not evident, and the scene looks realistic.	Although the model may be sturdy, construction materials such as glue and tape are easy to see, detracting somewhat from the realism of the scene.	Even though some parts of the model may be sturdy, other parts have fallen apart. Elements of the model have been hurriedly taped together.
Presentation	The model is highly attractive and detailed, although none of the details are extraneous. In dioramas, students render elements of the scene very realistically.	The model is attractive and includes many interesting details. Students draw and color elements of dioramas so that they are easy to understand.	The model adequately presents a scene. Most of the elements of dioramas are easy to make out or understand.	The model fails to present a scene adequately. Students pay little attention to color or shape when they make the elements of a diorama.

Activities and Projects

Answer Key

Discovery Activities About Geography

ACTIVITY ATLAS

What Kinds of Maps Does Geo Leo Need?

A. the population map
B. the vegetation map
C. the climate map

Bonus!

- A deciduous forest grows only in Afghanistan.
- The summer monsoons pass directly over the areas of tropical rain forest.

Analyze Density

1. Answers will vary. Possible answer: the coastal areas of North and South America, Europe, Asia.
2. Answers will vary. Possible answers: Australia, Africa, parts of South America; deserts and high mountain ranges.
3. Answers will vary. Students should recognize the factors that encourage high population density: mild climate, fertile soil, access to large bodies of water.
4. Answers will vary. Students should understand that physical features play an important role in influencing where people choose to live.

Bonus!

- Answers will vary. Students should be able to connect specific geographic features where they live to the population density.
- Answers will vary. Possible answers: a place with a mild climate and moderate rainfall, that is near an ocean and a large river, and that has a fertile plain for growing food and a population density of about 200 people per square mile. Accept all thoughtful answers.

Create a "Mental Map"
Bonus!

- Answers will vary. Students should realize that they probably included items that stand out in their memories and would be easily noticed by someone trying to follow the map.

The Earth's Seasons

ACTIVITY SHOP LAB

Procedure

Because of the tilt of the Earth's axis, the Northern Hemisphere gets less direct sunlight than the Southern Hemisphere during winter in the United States.

Observations

1. the angle at which the sun's rays hit the Earth. This is because the angle affects how much direct sunlight, or energy, hits a particular part of the Earth. The amount of direct sunlight is the main factor that affects the Earth's temperature.
2. summer. When it is winter in the Northern Hemisphere, the Earth is tilted so that the Southern Hemisphere is receiving more direct sunlight, which causes summer.
3. September 22. On this date, the tilt of the Earth makes both hemispheres receive about the same amount of direct sunlight.

Analysis and Conclusion

1. The seasons would not change. This is because all parts of the Earth would receive about the same amount of direct sunlight.
2. There would be no more seasons. The Earth would either travel closer to or farther away from the sun. In the first case, the temperature would get much warmer. In the second case, the temperature would get much colder.

A Five-Theme Tour

ACTIVITY SHOP INTERDISCIPLINARY

Decide Where You Will Go

a. Students should choose either a river or mountain tour.
b. Answers will vary. Students should choose five locations that are appropriate for their tour.

Describe the Places on Your Tour

a. Answers will vary. Descriptions should be accurate and informative.

Answer Key

b. Answers will vary. Students should demonstrate how the theme of human-environment interaction applies to each place on their tour.

Plan a Travel Route

a. Students should choose one place on their tour.
b. Students should write their home community as the starting point of the trip.
c. Students should find the mileage between each stop on the trip and compute the total miles. For example, if a trip is a tour up the Hudson River, students should indicate how many miles they would need to travel to get to New York City, and then how many miles the trip up and back down the river would total. Students might also decide to include the trip back to their home community in the total.

Learn About the Language

a. Students should fill in as many chart rows as needed with the languages spoken in the region of their trip location.
b. Students should indicate other places in the world where these languages are spoken.
c. Encourage students to fill in as much of the chart as possible. They should be able to find the words in foreign language dictionaries.

The Geography Game
BOOK PROJECT

A. Students should fill in the chart with information about the geography of different countries. The information should fit into the chart categories.
B. Students should use the chart information to create as many clue cards as they can.
C. Students play the game and tally the scores.

World News Today
BOOK PROJECT

A. Students should fill in the chart with information about the natural resources and economies of different countries and regions of the world. They should include information

about where they found articles and briefly summarize their content.
B. Students should use the table to keep track of the sources they use on the poster. Encourage students to view and learn from one another's posters.
C. Students should fill in the chart with the important points of their speech. Before they speak, they should go over the suggestions for giving a good speech.

Focus on Part of the Whole
BOOK PROJECT

A. Students should fill in the chart with information about physical characteristics, their effects on people, and other information for each region.
B. Students should fill in the chart with article titles and subjects and note where they located information.
C. Students create a wall map of a region or country, draw in physical features, and attach captions that explain the effects of land and climate on the population.

Desktop Countries
BOOK PROJECT

A. Students should fill in the chart with questions and responses from their interviews.
B. Students should list the ingredients for their dish on the page. They can use this list to answer questions about the dish that other students might have.
C. Students should use this page to help them create their desktop displays. Encourage students to think of their own ways to choose and display information.

Activities and Projects

Tests

TEST A

CHAPTER
1

The World of Geography

A. Key Terms

Directions: Fill in the blanks in Column I by writing the letter of the correct term from Column II. You will not use all the terms. *(10 points)*

Column I

_____ 1. Geographers identify imaginary east-west circles, or _____ lines around the globe.

_____ 2. Halfway between the North and the South poles, the _____ circles the globe.

_____ 3. The study of the Earth is called _____ .

_____ 4. The unit of measure used to determine an absolute location on a map or a globe is a(n) _____ .

_____ 5. A representation of the Earth's rounded surface on a flat piece of paper is called a(n) _____ .

Column II

a. cardinal direction

b. degree

c. Equator

d. geography

e. globe

f. latitude

g. meridian

h. projection

B. Key Concepts

Directions: Write the letter of the correct answer in each blank. *(45 points)*

_____ 6. Through their study of the Earth, geographers learn how the Earth and its people affect
  a. human health.
  b. the solar system.
  c. each other.
  d. political systems.

_____ 7. To learn more about the Earth, geographers organize information according to what themes?
  a. region, population, and place
  b. latitude, longitude, and movement
  c. location, population, and longitude
  d. location, place, human-environment interaction, movement, and regions

_____ 8. Which pair of basic questions guides geographers in their work?
  a. Where are things located? Why are they there?
  b. What is the climate? Why has it changed?
  c. When did the Earth form? What is it made from?
  d. Who lived where? When did they move?

© Prentice-Hall, Inc.

_____ 9. What do geographers learn by studying the theme of human-environment interaction?

 a. how people move from one region to another

 b. how cultural features define a location

 c. how people and the environment affect each other

 d. how regions differ from each other

_____ 10. Latitude and longitude lines help geographers identify

 a. absolute location.

 b. the depths of oceans.

 c. the Earth's distance from the sun.

 d. the heights of mountains.

_____ 11. The most accurate way to show the Earth's continents and bodies of water is with a

 a. Mercator projection.

 b. globe.

 c. Robinson projection.

 d. conformal map.

_____ 12. Which of the following statements explains why there are always distortions in a map?

 a. Maps are flat and the Earth is round.

 b. Small towns are hard to represent on a map.

 c. Mountains or plains don't show up on a map.

 d. Maps are too small to hold enough information.

_____ 13. A distorted map may change the shape of

 a. a globe.

 b. the Equator.

 c. the Prime Meridian.

 d. some landmasses.

_____ 14. The gaps in an interrupted projection map make it hard to

 a. carry in a back pack.

 b. determine the size of landmasses correctly.

 c. figure distances correctly.

 d. read borders clearly.

C. Critical Thinking

Directions: Answer the following questions on the back of this paper or on a separate sheet of paper. *(20 points)*

15. **Understanding Central Issues**   How do geographers use the theme of regions to organize information about the Earth?

16. **Making Comparisons**   What are some of the advantages and disadvantages of using only a map or only a globe to present information about the Earth?

D. Skill: Expressing Problems Clearly

Directions: The paragraph below discusses some of the problems with a Mercator projection. Read the paragraph and think about the problems. Then answer the questions in the space provided. *(25 points)*

When Mercator made his map, he had to make some decisions. He made sure that the shapes of the landmasses and ocean areas were similar to the shapes on a globe. But he had to stretch the spaces between the lines of longitude. This distorted the sizes of some of the landmasses on his map. Land near the Equator was about right, but land near the poles became much larger than it should be.

17. Would you be able to determine the true shape of landmasses and oceans by reading a Mercator projection? Why or why not?

_____

18. Would you be able to use a Mercator projection to determine the true size of a landmass near the Equator? Why or why not?

_____

19. Would you be able to use a Mercator projection to determine the true size of a landmass near the North Pole? Why or why not?

_____

20. Would you be able to use a Mercator projection to compare the sizes of different landmasses?

_____

21. Write a sentence that expresses the problem with a Mercator projection.

_____

The World of Geography

A. Key Terms

Directions: Match the definitions in Column I with the terms in Column II. Write the correct letter in each blank. You will not use all the terms. *(10 points)*

Column I

_____ **1.** the study of the Earth

_____ **2.** a type of imaginary line that circles the globe from north to south

_____ **3.** a change in the accuracy of shapes and distances

_____ **4.** a map feature that shows the four cardinal directions

_____ **5.** the section of a map that explains symbols for the map features

Column II

a. compass rose

b. distortion

c. Equator

d. geography

e. key

f. longitude

g. parallel

h. projection

B. Key Concepts

Directions: Write the letter of the correct answer in each blank. *(45 points)*

_____ **6.** Which of the following things would geographers be most likely to study?
    a. the moon
    b. the planets
    c. landforms and their locations
    d. chemicals and chemical reactions

_____ **7.** Geographers study how people
    a. and the Earth affect each other.
    b. interact with each other.
    c. and animals communicate.
    d. learn.

_____ **8.** What themes do geographers use to organize information?
    a. population and size of cities
    b. location, place, human-environment interaction, movement, and regions
    c. population and transportation
    d. climate and occupation

Tests

_____ **9.** Geographers are able to pinpoint the location of a place from east to west by using
   a. latitude lines.
   b. the Equator.
   c. longitude lines.
   d. parallel lines.

_____ **10.** Geographers study regions so that they can
   a. get people to move there.
   b. change the cultures.
   c. understand folk music.
   d. make comparisons between areas.

_____ **11.** A globe is more accurate than a map because a globe can show
   a. the true shapes of continents and oceans.
   b. city streets.
   c. a distorted view of the Earth.
   d. a particular region in great detail.

_____ **12.** Flat maps were invented because it was impossible to make a globe that was
   a. pretty enough for people to want.
   b. big enough to fit the oceans on.
   c. complete enough to use and convenient enough to carry.
   d. strong enough to last.

_____ **13.** Why do flat maps distort shapes of landmasses?
   a. No one is sure where the Equator really is.
   b. The Earth is round, not flat.
   c. The paper shrinks with time.
   d. Landmasses are always shifting.

_____ **14.** What is the best way to find out the subject of a map?
   a. Find the map key.
   b. Study the scale.
   c. Study the compass rose.
   d. Read the title.

C. Critical Thinking

Directions: Answer the following questions on the back of this paper or on a separate sheet of paper. *(20 points)*

15. Understanding Central Issues   Explain how the theme of movement helps geographers learn more about the Earth and its people.

16. Drawing Conclusions   If you were planning a two-day car trip to a different state, would you take a map or a globe to guide you? Explain your decision.

D. Skill: Expressing Problems Clearly

Directions: The paragraphs below discuss some of the problems with flat maps. Read the paragraphs and think about the problems. Then answer the questions in the spaces provided. *(25 points)*

Geographers call a Mercator projection a conformal map. It shows correct shapes but not true distances or sizes. Other mapmakers have used other techniques to try to draw an accurate map. For instance, an equal-area map shows the correct sizes of landmasses but their shapes are altered. The Peters projection is an equal-area map.

Mapmakers have tried other techniques. The interrupted projection is like the ripped peel of an orange. By creating gaps in the picture of the world, mapmakers have shown the size and shape of land accurately. But the gaps make it impossible to figure distances correctly. You could not use this projection to chart a course across an ocean.

17. What types of maps show the correct shapes of landmasses?

_____

18. What types of maps show the correct sizes of landmasses?

_____

19. What types of maps do not show correct distances?

_____

20. What type of map shows correct sizes, shapes, and distances?

_____

21. Write a sentence that expresses the problem with each type of map described in the paragraphs above.

_____

Tests

TEST A

Earth's Physical Geography

A. Key Terms

Directions: Match the definitions in Column I with the terms in Column II. Write the correct letter in each blank. You will not use all the terms. *(10 points)*

Column I

_____ **1.** the degree of hotness or coldness

_____ **2.** a thick blanket of gases that surrounds the Earth

_____ **3.** a huge piece of the outer skin of the Earth's crust

_____ **4.** plants that grow in an area naturally

_____ **5.** one trip of the Earth around the sun

Column II

a. atmosphere

b. plateau

c. plate

d. precipitation

e. revolution

f. temperature

g. vegetation

h. vertical climate

B. Key Concepts

Directions: Write the letter of the correct answer in each blank. *(45 points)*

_____ **6.** Why is the sun important to the planets in the solar system?
    a. It provides heat and light to the planets.
    b. It creates the gases that make up the planets.
    c. It orbits around the planets.
    d. It is close to the planets.

_____ **7.** One result of the Earth's tilt is that the Earth has
    a. winds.
    b. weather.
    c. seasons.
    d. daylight.

_____ **8.** Most of the Earth's surface is covered by
    a. mountains.
    b. plateaus.
    c. land.
    d. water.

_____ 9. As the huge pieces of the Earth's crust move, the Earth's surfaces
   a. collapse.   **c.** melt.
   b. change.   **d.** shrink.

_____ 10. The Earth's climate is affected by latitude, landforms, and a combination of
   a. ice and sand.   **c.** ocean depth and sea life.
   b. wind and water.   **d.** volcanoes and earthquakes.

_____ 11. The vegetation in a humid continental climate includes primarily
   a. forests and grasslands.   **c.** lichens and mosses.
   b. ice and snow.   **d.** different kinds of cacti.

_____ 12. There is a great deal of vegetation in a rain forest because there is
   a. a long winter.   **c.** a lot of sunlight and water.
   b. a cool, dry climate.   **d.** a vast tundra.

_____ 13. Where are moderate climates generally found?
   a. high in the mountains   **c.** in middle latitudes
   b. in low latitudes   **d.** near the Earth's poles

_____ 14. Without wind and water working together, the Earth would
   a. freeze.   **c.** overheat.
   b. stand still.   **d.** rotate.

C. Critical Thinking

Directions: Answer the following questions on the back of this paper or on a separate sheet of paper. *(20 points)*

15. **Recognizing Cause and Effect** How do the Earth's tilt and orbit cause the seasons to change?

16. **Distinguishing Fact From Opinion** Identify the kind of climate that you live in. Then write two facts and two opinions about that climate.

Tests

D. Skill: Using Geography Graphs

Directions: Use the graph below to answer the following questions. Write your answers in the blanks provided. *(25 points)*

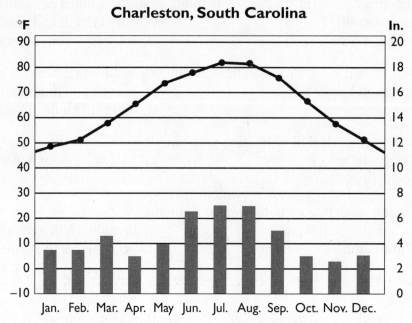

Charleston, South Carolina

Curved line shows temperatures in Fahrenheit degrees. Bars show precipitation in inches.

17. What is the coldest month of the year in Charleston? What is the hottest?

_____

18. Which months have the most precipitation in Charleston? Which month has the least?

_____

19. What appears to be the relationship between temperature and precipitation in Charleston?

_____

20. Between which months does the greatest increase in precipitation occur?

_____

21. According to this graph, how would you describe Charleston's climate—as moderate or polar?

_____

CHAPTER
2

Earth's Physical Geography

A. Key Terms

Directions: Complete each sentence in Column I by writing the letter of the correct term in Column II in the blank. You will not use all the terms. *(10 points)*

Column I

_____ **1.** Wide, flat areas near the coast are called lowlands, or_____ .

_____ **2.** The Earth moves around the sun on a path called a(n) _____ .

_____ **3.** The day-to-day changes in the air are called _____ .

_____ **4.** Life on the Earth is made possible because of the _____ , or surrounding blanket of gases.

_____ **5.** When scientists know information about a climate, they can predict what plants, or _____ , will grow there.

Column II

a. atmosphere

b. axis

c. orbit

d. plains

e. temperature

f. tundra

g. vegetation

h. weather

B. Key Concepts

Directions: Write the letter of the correct ending in each blank. *(45 points)*

_____ **6.** The Earth travels completely around the sun every
a. month.   **c.** year.
b. day.   **d.** two weeks.

_____ **7.** The amount of heat that the Northern and Southern hemispheres receive during the year depends on
a. the position of the moon.   **c.** the number of planets in the solar system.
b. the Earth's tilt.   **d.** the Equator.

_____ **8.** Mountains, plateaus, and plains are types of
a. plate tectonics.   **c.** magma.
b. landforms.   **d.** ridges.

Tests

_____ 9. The causes of weathering are
    a. erosion and plate movement.
    b. volcanoes and earthquakes.
    c. night and day.
    d. wind, rain, and ice.

_____ 10. What is one factor that influences the climate of an area?
    a. the positions of the planets
    b. the day of the week
    c. the size
    d. the latitude

_____ 11. One reason the Earth doesn't overheat is because of
    a. the movement of air.
    b. the position of the moon.
    c. the heights of mountains.
    d. the flatness of plains.

_____ 12. What are the major climate regions on Earth?
    a. hot and dry
    b. wet and cold
    c. mountainous and flat
    d. tropical, dry, moderate, continental, and polar

_____ 13. Thousands of kinds of plants grow in the rain forest because there is a good supply of
    a. heat, light, and water.
    b. farmers to plant crops.
    c. cool air currents.
    d. fertile soil.

_____ 14. Desert vegetation adapts to the hot environment by
    a. releasing a great deal of moisture.
    b. producing dense forests.
    c. producing flowers when the sun shines.
    d. releasing little moisture.

C. Critical Thinking

Directions: Answer the following questions on the back of this paper or on a separate sheet of paper. *(20 points)*

15. **Identifying Central Issues**   What are two major forces that shape and reshape the Earth? Describe how each force works.

16. **Recognizing Cause and Effect**   How have plants in continental and dry climates adapted to their environment?

D. Skill: Using Geography Graphs

Directions: Use the graph below to answer the following questions. Write your answers in the blanks. *(25 points)*

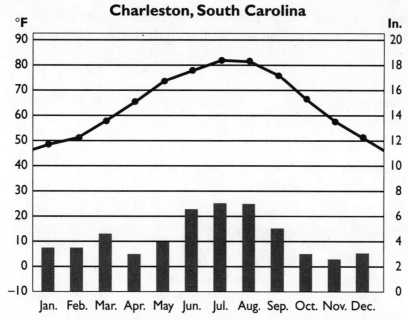

Charleston, South Carolina

Curved line shows temperatures in Fahrenheit degrees. **Bars** show precipitation in inches.

17. Which months have the most precipitation in Charleston? Which month has the least?

_____

18. What is the coldest month of the year in Charleston? What is the hottest?

_____

19. How much does the temperature change between August and September?

_____

20. Is Charleston's climate moderate or tropical?

_____

21. Between which months does the greatest increase in precipitation occur?

_____

Tests

TEST A

CHAPTER 3

Earth's Human Geography

A. Key Terms

Directions: Complete each sentence in Column I by writing the letter of the correct term from Column II in the blank. You will not use all the terms. *(10 points)*

Column I

_____ **1.** In a country with a high _____ , or total number of people, schools and public transportation can become overcrowded.

_____ **2.** A scientist who studies the people who live in certain areas is called a(n) _____ .

_____ **3.** A person who moves to a new country in order to settle there is called a(n) _____ .

_____ **4.** The number of live births each year per 1,000 people, or the _____ , varies from one country to another.

_____ **5.** When job opportunities appear in one region and disappear in another, a _____ , or mass movement of people may occur.

Column II

a. birthrate

b. demographer

c. immigrant

d. life expectancy

e. migration

f. population

g. "push-pull" theory

h. rural area

B. Key Concepts

Directions: Write the letter of the correct answer in each blank. *(45 points)*

_____ **6.** People tend to settle near places that have
   a. high mountains.
   b. extremely cold or hot climates.
   c. waterways that can be used for trade and travel.
   d. few natural resources.

_____ **7.** Why does the large continent of Australia have a relatively small population?
   a. Most of the country is covered by desert or dry grassland.
   b. Half of it is under water.
   c. There is too much swampy land.
   d. It is nearly covered in ice.

_____ **8.** Population density is the number of people that live in a region divided by
   a. the number of roads.
   b. the number of waterways.
   c. the number of square miles in the region.
   d. the number of people who used to live there.

_____ **9.** How do demographers figure out population growth?
  a. by studying the level of a water supply
  b. by comparing birthrates and death rates
  c. by counting all the new buildings
  d. by asking people how many children they have

_____ **10.** The world's population is rapidly increasing due to
  a. better health care.
  b. public transportation.
  c. global warming.
  d. the water supply.

_____ **11.** One serious problem caused by the growing population is
  a. a higher death rate.
  b. fewer available jobs.
  c. too much energy production.
  d. fewer medical advancements.

_____ **12.** The "push-pull" theory is used by scientists to explain
  a. how people fight.
  b. mountains.
  c. immigration.
  d. farming methods.

_____ **13.** Why did many people leave Ireland for the United States in the 1800s?
  a. They wanted to visit American cities.
  b. Ireland was experiencing a famine.
  c. They were escaping from religious persecution.
  d. There were too few schools in their native land.

_____ **14.** Large numbers of people have moved from rural areas to urban areas because they want to
  a. learn many languages.
  b. give their children more opportunities.
  c. live life at a slower pace.
  d. raise animals.

C. Critical Thinking

Directions: Answer the following questions on the back of this paper or on a separate sheet of paper. *(20 points)*

15. Identifying Central Issues On what continents do most of the world's people live? In your answer, list what factors cause people to settle in a particular place.

16. Comparing and Contrasting How does the growth of the world's population today compare with its growth 100 years ago?

D. Skill: Using Distribution Maps

Directions: Use the map below to answer the following questions. Write your answers in the blanks provided. *(25 points)*

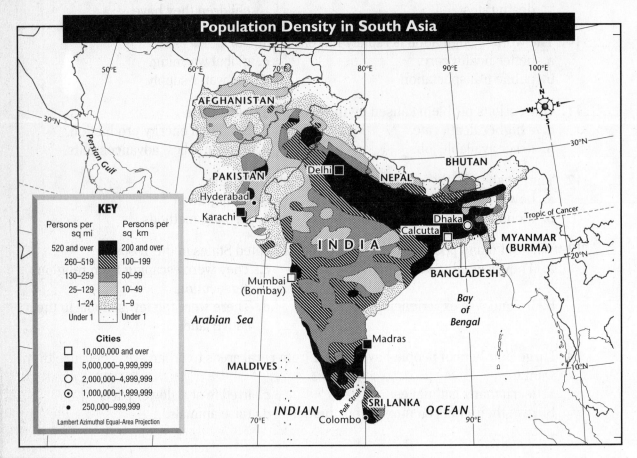

Population Density in South Asia

17. How is population represented on this map? _____

18. In general, how would you compare the population density of India with the

population density of Afghanistan? _____

_____

19. Is the population higher in Mumbai (Bombay) or Hyderabad? _____

20. What three countries have the highest population densities?

_____

21. What is the average population density in Sri Lanka? _____

Earth's Human Geography

A. Key Terms

Directions: Match the definitions in Column I with the terms in Column II. Write the correct letter in each blank. You will not use all the terms. *(10 points)*

Column I

_____ **1.** the way people are spread out over an area

_____ **2.** the movement of people to cities and the growth of cities

_____ **3.** the average number of years a person is expected to live

_____ **4.** a place where few people live

_____ **5.** the average number of people who live in a square mile of land

Column II

a. death rate

b. Green Revolution

c. life expectancy

d. population density

e. population distribution

f. "push-pull" theory

g. rural area

h. urbanization

B. Key Concepts

Directions: Write the letter of the correct answer in each blank. *(45 points)*

_____ **6.** What is one reason why more than 81 percent of the Earth's population lives in Asia, Europe, and North America?
   a. These continents are covered by rain forests.
   b. These continents have little rainfall.
   c. These continents have sources of fresh water.
   d. These continents have large deserts.

_____ **7.** Population distribution is uneven because people want to live in areas that have
   a. thick rain forests.
   b. extreme climates.
   c. dry grasslands.
   d. rich resources.

_____ **8.** A country that has a high population density has
   a. few people under 65 years old.
   b. a lot of land per person.
   c. some crowded areas.
   d. few urban areas.

Tests

_____ 9. By comparing birthrates and death rates, demographers figure out
   a. population density.
   b. where people are likely to move.
   c. population growth.
   d. why people migrate.

_____ 10. Because of an increase in food supply and better medical care, the world's population recently has
   a. remained the same.
   b. slowly decreased.
   c. made educational gains.
   d. rapidly increased.

_____ 11. One problem faced by the world's population today is
   a. too many jobs.
   b. not enough schools.
   c. a decline in foreign trade.
   d. a decrease in the use of natural resources.

_____ 12. To explain the reasons for immigration, demographers use
   a. life expectancies.
   b. birthrates and death rates.
   c. the "push-pull" theory.
   d. compasses.

_____ 13. Why did many people leave Vietnam for the United States?
   a. They knew that they spoke the same language.
   b. They didn't want to live under the new government.
   c. The cities in their country were too small.
   d. They preferred the warmer weather in the United States.

_____ 14. Many people leave the country for the city because they want
   a. to improve their health.
   b. to increase food production.
   c. to find jobs.
   d. to own land.

C. Critical Thinking

Directions: Answer the following questions on the back of this paper or on a separate sheet of paper. *(20 points)*

15. **Drawing Conclusions** What problems might result from the world's rapidly increasing population? Use facts from the chapter to support your conclusions.

16. **Identifying Central Issues** How does the "push-pull" theory explain immigration? In your answer, tell what the theory is.

D. Skill: Using Distribution Maps

Directions: Use the map below to answer the following questions. Write your answers in the blanks provided. *(25 points)*

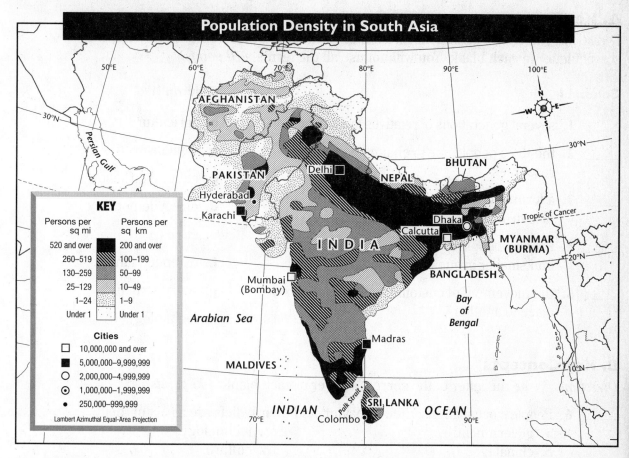

Population Density in South Asia

17. How does the key help you understand the information on the map? _____

_____

18. Name two countries that have areas with population densities of under one

person per square mile. _____

19. In general, how would you compare the population density of Sri Lanka

with the population density of Pakistan? _____

_____

20. What two cities have more than 10,000,000 people? _____

_____

21. What is the population density of Hyderabad? _____

TEST A

CHAPTER
4

Cultures of the World

A. Key Terms

Directions: Match the definitions in Column I with the terms in Column II. Write the correct letter in each blank. You will not use all the terms. *(10 points)*

Column I

_____ 1. several generations of relatives living together

_____ 2. the tools people use to change their natural resources

_____ 3. a form of government in which people participate directly in decision making

_____ 4. the way people in a culture are organized into smaller groups

_____ 5. the movement of customs and ideas from one place to another

Column II

a. agriculture

b. capitalism

c. cultural diffusion

d. direct democracy

e. ethics

f. extended family

g. social structure

h. technology

B. Key Concepts

Directions: Write the letter of the correct answer in each blank. *(45 points)*

_____ 6. People's occupations, their behavior, and their beliefs are a part of their
  a. government.
  b. climate.
  c. technology.
  d. culture.

_____ 7. When geographers study the theme of interaction, they learn
  a. how schools are run.
  b. how people and their environment affect each other.
  c. how agriculture develops.
  d. how the climate changes.

_____ 8. The social unit most responsible for teaching the customs and traditions of a culture is
  a. the family.
  b. the government.
  c. the army.
  d. the capitalists.

_____ 9. Three important features of a culture are
  a. weather, technology, and writing.   c. economy, population growth, and climate.
  b. language, values, and religious beliefs.   d. natural resources, landforms, and climate.

_____ 10. Communism, socialism, and capitalism are examples of
  a. political systems.   c. educational methods.
  b. economic systems.   d. technological achievements.

_____ 11. Three examples of forms of government are
  a. constitutional monarchy, dictatorship, and literature.   c. monarchy, extended family, and population.
  b. democracy, capitalism, and constitutional monarchy.   d. monarchy, democracy, and dictatorship.

_____ 12. Which of the following changes as a result of discoveries and inventions, shifts in the natural environment, and new ideas?
  a. culture   c. climate
  b. landforms   d. atmosphere

_____ 13. Communication around the world takes place quickly and easily because we live in a
  a. nuclear family.   c. global village.
  b. cultural landscape.   d. social structure.

_____ 14. The rapid exchange of ideas in the computer age has increased
  a. the growth of communism.   c. the rate of cultural change.
  b. the number of patriarchal families.   d. the number of constitutional monarchies.

C. Critical Thinking

Directions: Answer the following questions on the back of this paper or on a separate sheet of paper. *(20 points)*

15. **Comparing and Contrasting**   What are the similarities and the differences between a constitutional monarchy and rule by a dictator?

16. **Recognizing Cause and Effect**   Explain how technology can affect culture. Use an example in your explanation.

Tests

D. Skill: Locating Information

Directions: Imagine you are writing a report about Hong Kong. Refer to the pyramid of knowledge below to answer the following questions in the blanks provided. *(25 points)*

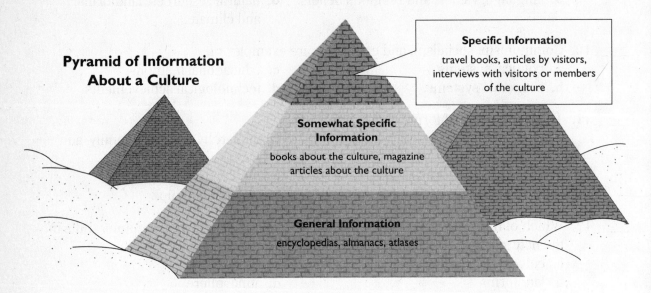

Pyramid of Information About a Culture

Specific Information
travel books, articles by visitors, interviews with visitors or members of the culture

Somewhat Specific Information
books about the culture, magazine articles about the culture

General Information
encyclopedias, almanacs, atlases

17. What kind of information should be found at the base of the pyramid?

_____

18. At what level of the pyramid would you put articles written by people who have visited Hong Kong and interviews with people who live there? Why?

_____

19. What sources would you use for the middle of the pyramid?

_____

20. When preparing your report, which level of the pyramid would you use first? Why?

_____

21. In general, how do you think the pyramid of knowledge can help you with your schoolwork?

_____

Cultures of the World

A. Key Terms

Directions: Complete each sentence in Column I by writing the letter of the correct term from Column II in the blank. You will not use all the terms. *(10 points)*

Column I

_____ 1. When one country accepts, borrows, or exchanges ideas with another, _____ takes place.

_____ 2. People can change their environment by using the _____ that is available to them.

_____ 3. A system for producing, distributing, and consuming wealth is called a(n) _____ .

_____ 4. In many industrial nations, such as the United States, parents and their children live in a(n) _____ .

_____ 5. Citizens elect certain people to make laws in a(n) _____ .

Column II

a. acculturation

b. cultural landscape

c. culture

d. economy

e. extended family

f. monarchy

g. nuclear family

h. representative democracy

i. technology

B. Key Concepts

Directions: Write the letter of the correct answer in each blank. *(45 points)*

_____ 6. The development of culture went through what stages?
a. early, middle, and late
b. the invention of tools, the discovery of fire, the growth of farming, and the use of writing
c. war and peace
d. the invention of the wheel, the beginning of dance, and the use of telescopes

_____ 7. What was it called when people went from hunting and gathering their foods to relying on farming and herding?
a. the age of discovery
b. the global village
c. the start of world history
d. the Agricultural Revolution

_____ 8. The most basic social unit of any culture is
a. the family.
b. the university.
c. the businesses.
d. the government.

Tests

_____ 9. Cultures in which women have the most authority in the family are called
   a. matriarchal.
   b. democratic.
   c. patriarchal.
   d. communist.

_____ 10. Three important features of a culture are
   a. natural resources, landforms, and climate.
   b. weather, technology, and writing.
   c. economy, population growth, and transportation.
   d. language, values, and religious beliefs.

_____ 11. What are the main economic systems in the world today?
   a. communism, capitalism, and democracy
   b. democracy, socialism, and constitutional monarchy
   c. communism, monarchy, and democracy
   d. communism, socialism, and capitalism

_____ 12. Democracy, monarchy, and dictatorship are examples of
   a. economic systems.
   b. kinds of social classes.
   c. forms of governments.
   d. kinds of families.

_____ 13. Changes in our natural environment, technological discoveries and inventions, and the spread of new ideas all cause
   a. population density changes.
   b. an economic depression.
   c. an economic inflation.
   d. cultural changes.

_____ 14. In a global village, people from all over the world can
   a. communicate quickly and easily.
   b. remain culturally isolated.
   c. limit cultural diffusion.
   d. influence government decision making.

C. Critical Thinking

Directions: Answer the following questions on the back of this paper or on a separate sheet of paper. *(20 points)*

15. **Comparing and Contrasting**   What are the similarities and the differences between a direct democracy and a representative democracy?

16. **Recognizing Cause and Effect**   Explain how a change in the environment can affect culture. Use an example in your explanation.

D. Skill: Locating Information

Directions: Imagine that you are writing a report about Senegal. Refer to the pyramid of knowledge below to answer the following questions in the blanks provided. *(25 points)*

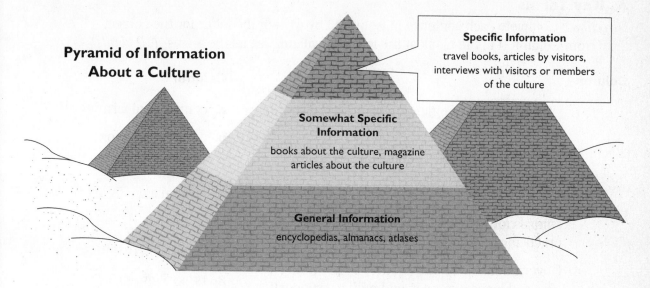

Pyramid of Information About a Culture

Specific Information
travel books, articles by visitors, interviews with visitors or members of the culture

Somewhat Specific Information
books about the culture, magazine articles about the culture

General Information
encyclopedias, almanacs, atlases

17. Where on the pyramid would you put information that you found in an atlas?

_____

18. Where would you put information you got from people who had lived in or visited Senegal? Why?

_____

19. From what kinds of sources would you get information to put in the middle level of the pyramid?

_____

20. Which level of the pyramid would provide the information you would use in the final stages of preparing your report? Why?

_____

21. In general, how do you think the pyramid of knowledge can help you with your schoolwork?

_____

Tests

TEST A

CHAPTER
5

Earth's Natural Resources

A. Key Terms

Directions: Complete each sentence in Column I by writing the letter for the correct term from Column II in the blank at the left. You will not use all the terms. *(10 points)*

Column I

_____ 1. Workers grow a single crop on a specialized farm called a(n) ____ .

_____ 2. A country with modern industries and a well-developed economy is called a(n) ____ .

_____ 3. When farmers raise only enough food and animals for their own families, they are practicing ____ .

_____ 4. Governments help one another by providing gifts and loans of money and military support called ____ .

_____ 5. A resource that can be replaced is a(n) ____ .

Column II

a. commercial farming

b. developed nation

c. developing nation

d. foreign aid

e. plantation

f. recyclable resource

g. renewable resource

h. subsistence farming

B. Key Concepts

Directions: Write the letter of the correct answer in each blank. *(45 points)*

_____ 6. A natural resource is any useful material that humans
    a. can make.
    b. cannot recycle.
    c. can find in developed countries.
    d. can find in the environment.

_____ 7. Minerals, coal, and natural gases are examples of
    a. renewable resources.
    b. second-level products.
    c. nonrenewable resources.
    d. synthetic materials.

_____ 8. Resources that were created over millions of years from the remains of prehistoric plants and animals are called
    a. manufactured resources.
    b. greenhouse gases.
    c. renewable resources.
    d. fossil fuels.

_____ 9. In the second stage of resource development, a person makes
   a. deliveries of products.
   b. products directly from natural resources.
   c. raw materials into things that people use.
   d. fossil fuels.

_____ 10. Because commercial farms use modern technology, a small number of workers can
   a. feed only the farmers' families.
   b. raise enough food for an entire country.
   c. turn a developed nation into an undeveloped one.
   d. live without goods and services.

_____ 11. What is one effect of the rapid population growth in developing countries?
   a. Food is being overproduced.
   b. Technological resources have expanded.
   c. Foreign aid is unnecessary.
   d. Resources are strained.

_____ 12. In South America, rain forests are most threatened by
   a. relocation.
   b. drought.
   c. acid rain.
   d. deforestation.

_____ 13. In order to reduce acid rain, Canada and the United States now have laws that require
   a. certain factories to reduce pollution.
   b. alternatives to ozone-destroying chemicals.
   c. the use of cheap energy sources.
   d. the protection of endangered species.

_____ 14. What is one cause of global warming?
   a. the use of hydroelectric power
   b. the burning of fossil fuels
   c. the use of pesticides
   d. subsistence farming

C. Critical Thinking

Directions: Answer the following questions on the back of this paper or on a separate sheet of paper. *(20 points)*

15. **Identifying Main Ideas** What are renewable resources? In your answer, give two examples of renewable resources.

16. **Drawing Conclusions** Which of the three stages of resource development do you think subsistence farmers participate in? In your answer, explain each stage of resource development.

D. Skill: Writing for a Purpose

Directions: Imagine that you are going to write an essay trying to persuade others to share your opinion on the subject of using fossil fuels. Read the selection below. Then answer the questions in the blanks provided. *(25 points)*

The summer of 1995 in New England was unusually hot and dry. Daytime temperatures stayed above 90 degrees for days on end. Heat and drought caused water shortages and killed crops. Some scientists feared this was the start of global warming, a slow increase in the Earth's temperature. Global warming may be caused by gases like carbon dioxide that are released into the air. They are called greenhouse gases. Developed countries produce about 75 percent of these gases. They are released when fossil fuels burn. These fuels produce most of the world's electricity. They also run the world's 550 million cars, buses, and trucks. Developing countries produce these gases when they burn forests to clear land and use wood for heating and cooking.

17. What is your opinion about the use of fossil fuels?

_____

18. With whom would you like to share your opinion? Why?

_____

19. What two reasons can you give to support your opinion?

_____

20. What is one fact that can support the reasons for your opinion?

_____

21. Write a sentence that would appeal to the emotions of your audience.

_____

Earth's Natural Resources

A. Key Terms

Directions: Match the definitions in Column I with the terms in Column II. Write the correct letter in each blank. You will not use all the terms. *(10 points)*

Column I

_____ **1.** a resource that can be replaced

_____ **2.** agricultural work done by companies that own huge farms

_____ **3.** a layer of gases in the upper part of our atmosphere

_____ **4.** a material in our environment that cannot be replaced

_____ **5.** a community of living things and their environment

Column II

a. commercial farming

b. deforestation

c. developing nation

d. ecosystem

e. nonrenewable resource

f. ozone

g. recyclable resource

h. renewable resource

B. Key Concepts

Directions: Write the letter of the correct answer in each blank. *(45 points)*

_____ **6.** Soil, water, and minerals are examples of
    a. fossil fuels.
    b. vegetation.
    c. natural resources.
    d. synthetic resources.

_____ **7.** Two examples of nonrenewable resources are
    a. corn and wheat.
    b. coal and natural gas.
    c. pigs and goats.
    d. wind and water.

_____ **8.** Materials created over millions of years from the remains of prehistoric plants and animals are
    a. manufactured resources.
    b. synthetic resources.
    c. renewable resources.
    d. fossil fuels.

Tests

_____ **9.** What is the first stage of resource development?
    a. making raw materials into things that people use
    b. using the land and resources directly to make products
    c. distributing products to people who want them
    d. creating communications systems

_____ **10.** Countries with little industry are called
    a. industrialized nations.
    b. prehistoric nations.
    c. developed nations.
    d. developing nations.

_____ **11.** Subsistence farms raise enough food to
    a. feed only the farmers' families.
    b. feed an entire country.
    c. export food to other countries.
    d. turn a developing nation into a developed one.

_____ **12.** As a result of their rapid growth in population, many developing countries are
    a. decreasing foreign aid.
    b. using renewable resources.
    c. straining their resources.
    d. limiting their pollution.

_____ **13.** Global warming may be caused by the use of
    a. solar energy.
    b. fossil fuels.
    c. hydroelectric power.
    d. recyclable materials.

_____ **14.** Fertilizer, pesticides, and waste products are substances that
    a. produce acid rain.
    b. create greenhouse gases.
    c. encourage commercial farming.
    d. pollute the water.

C. Critical Thinking

Directions: Answer the following questions on the back of this paper or on a separate sheet of paper. *(20 points)*

15. Identifying Main Ideas   What are nonrenewable resources? In your answer, give two examples of nonrenewable resources.

16. Drawing Conclusions   Which of the three stages of resource development do you think is most common in the United States? In your answer, explain each stage of resource development.

D. Skill: Writing for a Purpose

Directions: Imagine that you are going to write an essay trying to persuade others to share your opinion on the subject of endangered species. Read the selection below. Then answer the questions in the blanks provided. (*25 points*)

Extinction has many causes. People may build houses or businesses on land that is the habitat of particular animals or plants. The air, soil, or water may be too polluted for a species of plant or animal to survive. Sometimes, a species is hunted until it disappears. Usually, more than one thing endangers a species. The goal of the Endangered Species Act is to stop extinction. But people disagree about the law. Some think that humans should be allowed to use natural resources as they need them. Others think people should stop doing things that hurt other species.

17. What is your opinion about government efforts to protect endangered species?

_____

18. With whom would you like to share your opinion? Why?

_____

19. What two reasons can you give to support your opinion?

_____

20. What is one fact that can support the reasons for your opinion?

_____

21. Write a sentence that might appeal to the emotions of your audience.

_____

Tests

Geography: Tools and Concepts

A. Key Terms

Directions: Match the definitions in Column I with the terms in Column II. Write the correct letter in each blank. You will not use all the terms. *(10 points)*

Column I

_____ **1.** the way of life of a group of people who share similar beliefs or customs

_____ **2.** a country with little industry

_____ **3.** the average number of people who live in a square mile of land

_____ **4.** any useful material found in the environment

_____ **5.** an oval-shaped path around the sun

Column II

a. culture

b. demographer

c. developed nation

d. developing nation

e. natural resource

f. orbit

g. population density

h. recyclable resource

i. social structure

B. Key Concepts

Directions: Write the letter of the correct answer in each blank. *(45 points)*

_____ **6.** What are three of the five themes that geographers use to study the Earth?
  a. meridians, geography, and culture
  b. regions, hemispheres, and latitude
  c. location, place, and movement
  d. parallels, longitude, and latitude

_____ **7.** Why are flat maps sometimes used instead of globes?
  a. Globes are too inaccurate to show the Earth as it is.
  b. Globes are not detailed enough for all uses.
  c. Globes are not the same shape as the Earth.
  d. Globes are too difficult to manufacture.

_____ **8.** Seasons change because of the Earth's
  a. rotation.
  b. continents and oceans.
  c. atmosphere.
  d. tilt and orbit.

_____ **9.** What are the Earth's major climate regions?
   a. prairie, plateau, and dry
   b. summer, fall, winter, and spring

   c. tropical, dry, moderate, continental, and polar
   d. Equator, rain forest, and grassland

_____ **10.** Most of the Earth's population lives in
   a. Asia, Europe, and North America.
   b. Australia, Europe, and North America.

   c. the Caribbean and Australia.
   d. South America.

_____ **11.** Demographers use the "push-pull" theory to explain
   a. where people farm.
   b. how people live.

   c. why people migrate.
   d. when people began to trade.

_____ **12.** Three important features of a culture are
   a. vegetation, climate, and seasonal change.
   b. language, values, and religious beliefs.

   c. population density, economy, and industry.
   d. industry, agriculture, and natural resources.

_____ **13.** Socialism, communism, and capitalism are the three major
   a. systems of government.
   b. economic systems.

   c. cultures.
   d. social structures.

_____ **14.** What is the first step that cultures take in working with resources?
   a. distributing products to people who want them
   b. processing raw materials into finished products

   c. using fossil fuels to heat homes
   d. using land and resources directly to make products

C. Critical Thinking

Directions: Answer the following questions on the back of this paper or on a separate sheet of paper. (*20 points*)

15. Understanding Central Issues   Why do you think geographers are interested in the effect that the environment has on culture and the effects that people have on their environment? In your answer, define what culture is and explain its relationship to the surrounding environment.

16. Drawing Conclusions   Name and describe the five themes of geography.

D. Skill: Locating Information

Directions: Imagine that you are writing a report about how to live in the Andes Mountains in South America. You have the following sources of information available: encyclopedias, maps, interviews with local people, travel books about South America, books and magazines about the Andes Mountains. Think about the information you would need to complete the assignment. Then answer the questions in the blanks provided. *(25 points)*

17. What are two sources of general information that you would use in your report?

_____

18. What are two sources of very specific information you would use?

_____

19. What are two sources of somewhat specific information you would use?

_____

20. What information would you find first, second, and third?

_____

21. If you were building a "pyramid of knowledge," what information would you put on the base level, the middle level, and the top level?

_____

Geography: Tools and Concepts

A. Key Terms

Directions: Complete each sentence in Column I by writing the letter for the correct term from Column II in the blank at the left. You will not use all the terms. *(10 points)*

Column I

_____ 1. A community of living things and their environment is called a(n) _____ .

_____ 2. In some cultures, several generations of relatives live together in a(n) _____ .

_____ 3. A resource that has to be altered or changed before being used is called a(n) _____ .

_____ 4. Every 24 hours the Earth completes one _____ on its axis.

_____ 5. A characteristic behavior of a people, such as a language, skill, or custom passed from one generation to another, is called a(n) _____ .

Column II

a. acid rain

b. cultural trait

c. deforestation

d. ecosystem

e. extended family

f. geography

g. population distribution

h. raw material

i. rotation

B. Key Concepts

Directions: Write the letter of the correct answer in each blank. *(45 points)*

_____ 6. Three of the five themes that geographers use to study the Earth are
   a. culture, resources, and population.
   b. weather, climate, and resources.
   c. hemisphere, vegetation, and climate.
   d. regions, movement, and human-environment interaction.

_____ 7. What special features help people understand the information on maps?
   a. projection and distortion
   b. compass rose, key, and scale
   c. columns, rows, and diagonals
   d. rotation, distortion, and tilt

_____ 8. When the North Pole tilts toward the sun, the Northern Hemisphere experiences
   a. more darkness.
   b. the same season as the Southern Hemisphere.
   c. autumn.
   d. summer.

Tests

_____ 9. Millions of years ago Pangaea, a huge landmass, split into
     a. the seven seas.
     b. the Rocky Mountains.
     c. separate continents.
     d. separate ocean floors.

_____ 10. Which three continents have a relatively small population?
     a. Asia, Europe, and North America
     b. South America, North America, and Australia
     c. Africa, Asia, and North America
     d. Australia, Africa, and South America

_____ 11. The world's population is increasing because
     a. the Industrial Revolution took place.
     b. the Green Revolution took place.
     c. the food supply increased and medical care improved.
     d. the birthrate and death rate are now equal.

_____ 12. The basic social unit in any culture is
     a. the family.
     b. the school.
     c. the government.
     d. the community.

_____ 13. Minerals, oil, and coal are examples of
     a. nonrenewable resources.
     b. renewable resources.
     c. manufactured resources.
     d. technological resources.

_____ 14. One result of the Industrial Revolution was that countries were split into
     a. North and South America.
     b. developed and developing nations.
     c. socialist and capitalist nations.
     d. democracies and dictatorships.

C. Critical Thinking

Directions: Answer the following questions on the back of this paper or on a separate sheet of paper. *(20 points)*

15. **Expressing Problems Clearly** What are three major problems caused by the tremendous increase in world population in recent years?

16. **Recognizing Cause and Effect** Identify two environmental problems and describe their causes.

D. Skill: Locating Information

Directions: Imagine that you are writing a report about how people in the United States are protecting endangered species. You have the following information available: map of the United States, statistics on endangered species, article on laws passed to protect endangered species, Internet site that describes animal characteristics, biography of a woman who started a shelter to treat and release injured birds, and magazine and newspaper articles about environmental action groups. Think about the information you need to complete the assignment. Then answer the questions in the blanks provided. *(25 points)*

17. What are two sources of general information that you would use in your report?

_____

18. What are two sources of very specific information you would use?

_____

19. What are two sources of somewhat specific information you would use?

_____

20. What information would you find first, second, and third?

_____

21. If you were building a "pyramid of knowledge," what information would you put on the base level, the middle level, and the top level?

_____

Answer Key

Chapter 1

Test A

1. f **2.** c **3.** d **4.** b **5.** h
6. c **7.** d **8.** a **9.** c **10.** a
11. b **12.** a **13.** d **14.** c

15. Answers may vary. Possible answer: The theme of regions allows comparisons to be made between areas that share certain similarities in things such as land and climate.

16. Answers may vary. Possible answer: Because a globe is round, like the Earth, it shows the continents and oceans much as they really are, although to scale. However, it's impossible to make a globe complete enough for people to use and small enough to be convenient, which is why maps are sometimes more useful. Maps, however, show land with some distortion.

17. yes, because the shapes of landmasses and ocean areas are similar to those on a globe

18. yes, because land near the Equator is not very distorted on this map

19. no, because the size of land near the poles is very distorted

20. no, because while land near the Equator is shown accurately, the landmasses near the poles are shown as being much larger than they really are

21. Answers may vary. One possible response: Although a Mercator map can be used to determine the shapes of oceans and landmasses and the sizes of areas close to the Equator, it distorts the sizes of areas near the poles.

Test B

1. d **2.** f **3.** b **4.** a **5.** e
6. c **7.** a **8.** b **9.** c **10.** d
11. a **12.** c **13.** b **14.** d

15. Answers may vary. Possible answer: Movement concerns the relationships among different places, including how movement changes the cultural environment.

16. Answers may vary. Possible answer: I would take a map. Maps are easy to carry and can give the kind of detailed information, such as highway exits and road signs, that would be useful on a car trip. Globes are more difficult to travel with and do not provide detailed information.

17. conformal (or Mercator projection) maps and interrupted projection maps

18. equal-area (or Peters projection) maps and interrupted projection maps

19. Mercator and interrupted projection maps

20. none of them

21. Answers may vary. Possible answer: Neither conformal maps, equal-area maps, nor interrupted projection maps can show the correct sizes and shapes of, and distances between, the Earth's landmasses.

Chapter 2

Test A

1. f **2.** a **3.** c **4.** g **5.** e
6. a **7.** c **8.** d **9.** b **10.** b
11. a **12.** c **13.** c **14.** c

15. Answers may vary. Possible answer: The Earth's tilt and orbit affect the way temperatures change during seasons. The amount of heat that a part of the planet receives depends on the planet's tilt. When the North Pole tilts toward the sun, the Northern Hemisphere receives more direct sunlight, so it is summer there. At the same time, the Southern Hemisphere receives less direct sunlight, so it's cooler and the season is winter there.

16. Answers will vary. Possible answer: Facts—Moderate climates have a wide variety of vegetation. They are found in middle latitudes. Opinions—Moderate climates are the best climates. People in moderate climates are happier than people in polar climates.

17. The coldest month is January. The hottest month is July.

18. July and August have the most precipitation. November has the least.

Answer Key

19. The hottest months have the most precipitation.

20. The greatest increase occurs between May and June.

21. Charleston has a moderate climate.

Test B

1. d   **2.** c   **3.** h   **4.** a   **5.** g

6. c   **7.** b   **8.** b   **9.** d   **10.** d

11. a   **12.** d   **13.** a   **14.** d

15. Answers will vary. Possible answer: Plate tectonics shape the landmasses of the Earth because as the Earth's plates move, the shape of the Earth's surface is altered. Volcanoes shape the landmasses of the Earth because when the molten rock that explodes out of them cools, it creates new land.

16. Answers may vary. Possible answer: In the humid continental climate, summer temperatures are moderate, and winters can be cold. Vegetation grows during warmer parts of the year. Vegetation in deserts and other dry places have adaptations that prevent loss of water.

17. July and August have the most precipitation. October has the least.

18. The coldest month is January. The hottest month is July.

19. The temperature drops 5 degrees between August and September.

20. Charleston has a moderate climate.

21. The greatest increase occurs between May and June.

Chapter 3

Test A

1. f   **2.** b   **3.** c   **4.** a   **5.** e

6. c   **7.** a   **8.** c   **9.** b   **10.** a

11. b   **12.** c   **13.** b   **14.** b

15. Answers may vary. Possible answer: Most of the world's population lives in Asia, Europe, and North America. People tend to settle where there are natural resources, waterways, and climates that are neither too hot nor too cold.

16. Answers may vary. Possible answer: One hundred years ago, the world's population was growing more slowly than it is today. One hundred years ago, farmers worked without modern machinery, and food supplies were scarce; more people died of diseases because fewer medicines were available; and the death rate was higher than the birthrate. Today, the world's population is soaring, largely because scientific methods have increased the world's food supply, and medical advances have increased the number of babies who live at birth and the number of years people live.

17. different patterns

18. India is an area of high population density; fewer people live in Afghanistan.

19. Mumbai (Bombay)

20. India, Sri Lanka, and Bangladesh

21. 260–519 people per square mile

Test B

1. e   **2.** h   **3.** c   **4.** g   **5.** d

6. c   **7.** d   **8.** c   **9.** c   **10.** d

11. b   **12.** c   **13.** b   **14.** c

15. Answers may vary. Possible answer: The rapid growth in the world's population has led to serious problems for many poorer nations. These problems have arisen because in some parts of the world, there isn't enough food or water; there isn't enough money to import goods; people can't find jobs; there are too few schools; adequate housing is scarce and expensive; and transportation and sanitation are inadequate.

16. Answers may vary. Possible answer: The "push-pull" theory is used to explain why people leave their homes and move to another country. According to this theory, people migrate because certain things, such as economic or political reasons, "push" them to leave. Similarly, people can be "pulled" to migrate to another country because of factors such as better living conditions or a culture, climate, and vegetation similar to those found in their native lands.

17. It explains how patterns on the map relate to the area's population density.

Tests

Answer Key

18. Afghanistan, Pakistan, India, Nepal, or Bhutan
19. Sri Lanka has more areas with high population densities than Pakistan does.
20. Mumbai (Bombay) and Calcutta
21. 25–129 people per square mile

Chapter 4

Test A

1. f	**2.** h	**3.** d	**4.** g	**5.** c
6. d	**7.** b	**8.** a	**9.** b	**10.** b
11. d	**12.** a	**13.** c	**14.** c	

15. Answers will vary. Possible answer: In both forms of government, a single person is the most important person in the government. However, in a constitutional monarchy, the king or queen is often only a symbol of the country. Their actual power is limited by a constitution. A constitution sets laws and determines the government's power. In a country ruled by a dictator, there is no constitution to limit the dictator. The dictator has total power over the country.
16. Answers will vary. Possible answer: Technology affects culture by causing cultural change. For example, computers change how and where people work.
17. general information
18. I would put this information at the top level because this is very specific material.
19. I would use sources that give somewhat specific information, such as books and magazine articles about the culture.
20. I would use the bottom level first, because I would want to start with general information.
21. It can be used with an assignment that requires research about a specific topic.

Test B

1. a	**2.** i	**3.** d	**4.** g	**5.** h
6. b	**7.** d	**8.** a	**9.** a	**10.** d
11. d	**12.** c	**13.** d	**14.** a	

15. Answers will vary. Possible answer: In both kinds of democracy, people have a voice in how things are run. In a direct democracy, everyone participates in running the country's affairs. In a representative democracy, citizens elect people to run the country's affairs.
16. Answers will vary. Possible answer: A change in environment can affect the way people work, eat, and dress. For example, if the climate becomes much colder, people may start to wear heavier, warmer clothing.
17. This information would go in the bottom level of the pyramid.
18. I would put this at the top of the pyramid because it is the most specific information.
19. Books and magazine articles about the culture would provide the information for the middle level of the pyramid.
20. I would use the information in the top level last because that is the most specific information.
21. It can be used with an assignment that requires research about a specific topic.

Chapter 5

Test A

1. e	**2.** b	**3.** h	**4.** d	**5.** g
6. d	**7.** c	**8.** d	**9.** c	**10.** b
11. d	**12.** d	**13.** a	**14.** b	

15. Answers may vary. Possible answer: A renewable resource is one that can be replaced, such as a tree, an animal, and other living things.
16. Answers may vary. Possible answer: In the first stage, people use land and resources directly to make products. In the second stage, people make raw materials into things they can use by manufacturing them. In the third stage, people distribute the products they make to the consumers who need them. This involves the development of service industries, including transportation and communications. I think that subsistence farmers participate in the first stage of resource development. They use land to make food.
17. Answers will vary. Possible answer: I think that the government should spend money to find more fossil fuels, not to get rid of them.

Answer Key

18. Answers will vary. Possible answer: I would like to share my opinion with my senator because she can vote on laws concerning fossil fuels.

19. Answers will vary. Possible answer: Fossil fuels are very important to the world's economy. Scientists aren't sure whether fossil fuels cause global warming.

20. Answers may vary. Possible answer: 550 million cars run on fossil fuels.

21. Answers may vary. Possible answer: Concern over a problem that may not even exist could endanger the American way of life.

Test B

1. h	**2.** a	**3.** f	**4.** e	**5.** d
6. c	**7.** b	**8.** d	**9.** b	**10.** d
11. a	**12.** c	**13.** b	**14.** d	

15. Answers may vary. Possible answer: A nonrenewable resource is one that cannot be replaced once it is used up. Oil and coal are two examples of nonrenewable resources.

16. Answers may vary. Possible answer: In the first stage, people use land and resources directly to make products. In the second stage, people make raw materials into things they can use by manufacturing them. In the third stage, people distribute the products they make to the consumers who need them. This involves the development of service industries, including transportation and communications. The third stage of development is probably most common in the U.S.

17. Answers will vary. Possible answer: I think that the government is doing the right thing.

18. Answers will vary. Possible answer: I would like to share my opinion with my senator because she can vote on laws to protect endangered species.

19. Answers will vary. Possible answer: If these animals aren't protected they will die out, which may upset the ecosystem. Also, people should be discouraged from destroying the environment.

20. Answers may vary. Possible answer: The fact that pollution is one cause of extinction supports the fact that people will destroy the environment unless there are laws against it.

21. Answers may vary. Possible answer: As a young American, I am concerned about the way we treat the other species that share this country with us.

Final Exam

Test A

1. a	**2.** d	**3.** g	**4.** e	**5.** f
6. c	**7.** b	**8.** d	**9.** c	**10.** a
11. c	**12.** b	**13.** b	**14.** d	

15. Answers may vary. A possible answer: Culture is the way of life of a group of people who share similar values and beliefs. Geographers want to know how the environment, including climate, vegetation, and available resources, affects culture. They're also interested in how people use technology to change their surroundings. This interaction between people and the environment is important because it affects everything that makes up the culture of a region, including the food people eat, the houses they live in, and the kinds of work they do.

16. Answers may vary. Possible answer: The five themes are location, which enables geographers to identify absolute and relative locations; place, which includes the natural and cultural features of a location; human-envronment interaction, which shows how the environment and people affect one another; movement, which explains the relationship between places; and regions, which is used to make comparisons. These five themes are important because they enable geographers to organize the information they find about a particular place.

17. an encyclopedia article about South America; an atlas map of South America

18. travel books about the Andes region of South America; interviews with people who have lived in or visited the area

19. a book about the culture of South America; magazine articles about the Andes Mountains

Answer Key

20. general information; somewhat specific information; very specific information

21. general information on the base level, somewhat specific information on the middle level, very specific information on the top level

Test B

1. d   **2.** e   **3.** h   **4.** i   **5.** b
6. d   **7.** b   **8.** d   **9.** c   **10.** d
11. c   **12.** a   **13.** a   **14.** b

15. Answers may vary. Possible answer: One of the problems caused by the increase in the world's population is that more resources are being used, which leads to shortages of fresh water, energy, and food supplies. Also, there aren't enough jobs to support the growing population, and there aren't enough services, like education, transportation, and sanitation, to ensure everyone a decent standard of living.

16. Answers may vary. A possible answer: One environmental problem is acid rain, which has caused great damage to the forests of New York. Acid rain is produced when the chemicals released by cars and industries combine with water vapor in the air. Another environmental problem is river and sewage pollution, which can destroy living things in the water and endanger people. This pollution is caused by people dumping waste into the waters and by fertilizers and pesticides that farmers use.

17. an encyclopedia article about endangered species; an atlas map of the United States

18. an interview with a person who works with endangered species; an article by someone who has passed laws to protect species

19. a book about endangered species; a magazine article about efforts to protect animals

20. general information; somewhat specific information; very specific information

21. general information on the base level, somewhat specific information on the middle level, very specific information on the top level

Spanish Support

CARTAS PARA LA FAMILIA

El mundo de la geografía

La Línea Abierta de Ciencias Sociales

Querida familia:

Durante las próximas semanas, en nuestra clase de ciencias sociales estudiaremos la geografía. Observaremos detenidamente nuestro planeta y sus habitantes. En el Capítulo 1, estudiaremos los cinco temas principales de la geografía: la ubicación, el lugar, la interacción de los seres humanos con el medio ambiente, los desplazamientos y las regiones del planeta. Algunos de nuestros estudios incluirán: los climas y las formaciones físicas, las poblaciones y las culturas humanas, y los recursos naturales. Si usted tiene experiencia o información específica sobre la geografía, por favor compártala con su hijo o hija.

Vamos a estudiar cómo los geógrafos hallan ubicaciones exactas y cómo varían las características físicas de un lugar a otro. También vamos a aprender sobre los distintos tipos de mapas que existen. Una buena manera de aprender sobre el contenido de este capítulo es observando un mapa o un globo terráqueo con su hijo o hija. Además vamos a aprender a leer los signos convencionales (o las inscripciones) de los mapas, para identificar la escala y para comprender cómo los mapas en superficies planas pueden representar formas y distancias de una manera inexacta. Cuando camine o maneje por el vecindario, es posible que observe algunos lugares importantes que podrían estar representados en un mapa local. Pida a su hijo o hija que haga un mapa local o una lista de los lugares de interés que haya cerca de donde viven.

Si lee un periódico con su hijo o hija, pueden hablar de los patrones del tiempo y el clima en su región—ambas partes importantes de la geografía local. Podría también contar historias de distintos aspectos de la geografía alrededor del mundo, así como de sitios de interés o del desplazamiento de personas de un país a otro. También puede señalar maneras en que los seres humanos estamos afectando el medio ambiente.

Esté atento a recibir noticias sobre los estudios de geografía de nuestra clase. Espero que tanto usted como su hijo o hija disfruten al compartir el estudio de la geografía.

Atentamente,

CAPÍTULO 1
**El mundo
de la geografía**

Los cinco temas de la geografía

A. Durante la lectura

Instrucciones: A medida que vayas leyendo la Sección 1, contesta las siguientes preguntas en los espacios en blanco.

1. ¿Cuáles son las dos preguntas que los geógrafos tratan de contestar al estudiar distintos lugares?

_____

2. ¿De qué manera las cinco materias (la ubicación, el lugar, la interacción del ser humano con el medio ambiente, los desplazamientos y las regiones del planeta) les ayudan a los geógrafos a estudiar nuestro planeta?

_____

3. ¿Cuáles son dos maneras de describir una ubicación?

_____

4. Cuando se explica que un río está a 250 millas al norte de San Antonio, ¿qué manera de describir la ubicación se está usando?

_____

5. ¿Por qué el estudio de los desplazamientos es importante para los geógrafos?

_____

B. Repaso de los términos clave

Instrucciones: Para completar cada oración, escribe el término correspondiente en el espacio en blanco.

6. El estudio de la Tierra y sus habitantes se llama _____ .

7. Una línea imaginaria que rodea la Tierra de este a oeste se llama tanto _____ como

_____ .

8. Una línea imaginaria que rodea la Tierra del Polo Norte al Polo Sur se llama tanto

_____ como _____ .

9. Los geógrafos miden ubicaciones al este y al oeste de _____ , al cual se le ha asignado 0 grados.

10. El paralelo en la mitad del globo terráqueo es _____ .

11. La unidad de medida que usan los geógrafos para medir las ubicaciones en los mapas es

_____ .

Spanish Support

EXAMEN DE LA SECCIÓN

CAPÍTULO 1
El mundo
de la geografía

Los cinco temas de la geografía

A. Términos y conceptos clave

Instrucciones: Lee las oraciones a continuación. Si una oración es verdadera, escribe V en el espacio en blanco. Si es falsa, escribe F. En otra hoja de papel, vuelve a escribir las oraciones falsas para convertirlas en verdaderas.

_____ **1.** El Meridiano Principal pasa por Greenwich, Inglaterra.

_____ **2.** Las líneas de longitud rodean la Tierra formando círculos paralelos a la línea ecuatorial.

_____ **3.** La línea ecuatorial es una línea imaginaria que rodea el globo terráqueo por su zona más ancha.

_____ **4.** La geografía es el estudio de la Tierra.

_____ **5.** Las líneas de latitud dividen el globo terráqueo en unidades llamadas polos.

B. Ideas principales

Instrucciones: En cada espacio en blanco, escribe la letra que mejor conteste la pregunta.

_____ **6.** Los geógrafos estudian muchas cosas, incluyendo: los océanos, la vida de las plantas, los accidentes geográficos y
  a. la geometría.
  b. los cometas.
  c. las personas.
  d. los asteroides.

_____ **7.** Los geógrafos usan los cinco temas de la geografía para
  a. estudiar la historia del mundo.
  b. organizar información.
  c. estudiar la música del mundo.
  d. medir las ubicaciones.

_____ **8.** Para determinar la ubicación exacta de un lugar, los geógrafos usan
  a. los accidentes geográficos cercanos.
  b. el Océano Atlántico y el Océano Pacífico.
  c. el Polo Norte y el Polo Sur.
  d. la latitud y la longitud.

_____ **9.** ¿Qué les ayuda a comprender a los geógrafos el tema de los desplazamientos?
  a. las características físicas y humanas de una ubicación
  b. cómo las personas, los productos y las ideas van de un lugar a otro
  c. qué tan lejos está un lugar de la línea ecuatorial
  d. el clima de un lugar

_____ **10.** ¿Para qué usan los geógrafos el tema de las regiones?
  a. para hacer comparaciones
  b. para identificar las rutas comerciales
  c. para ubicar lugares
  d. para mostrar cómo afectamos los seres humanos el medio ambiente

CAPÍTULO 1
El mundo de la geografía

Las herramientas de los geógrafos

A. Durante la lectura

Instrucciones: A medida que vayas leyendo la Sección 2, completa la tabla a continuación. Debajo de cada idea principal, escribe dos ideas que la apoyen.

Idea principal A
Hace mucho tiempo, eran pocas las personas que sabían lo que sucedía con la tierra y el agua más allá de sus viviendas y vecindarios.
1. _____ _____
2. _____ _____

Idea principal B
Los globos terráqueos son una buena manera de presentar información sobre la Tierra, pero los mapas planos, por lo general, son una mejor manera de representar la Tierra.
3. _____ _____
4. _____ _____

B. Repaso de los términos clave

Instrucciones: Para completar cada oración, escribe el término correspondiente en el espacio en blanco.

5. Cuando una masa de tierra se ve más grande en un mapa que en un globo terráqueo, el cambio en la

   figura se llama _____ .

6. Los símbolos que aparecen en un mapa están explicados en _____ o inscripciones.

7. Una bola redonda llamada _____ muestra a la Tierra en un tamaño más pequeño o

   _____ .

8. Los geógrafos llaman un mapa conforme a _____ de Mercator.

9. Un mapa por lo general tiene _____ que muestra _____ , que son
   norte, sur, este y oeste.

Spanish Support

Nombre _____ Clase _____ Fecha _____

Las herramientas de los geógrafos

A. Términos y conceptos clave

Instrucciones: Empareja las definiciones de la Columna I con los términos de la Columna II. Escribe la letra correspondiente en cada espacio en blanco.

Columna I

_____ **1.** Una representación de la Tierra en una hoja de papel es _____ .

_____ **2.** El modelo esférico de la Tierra se llama _____ .

_____ **3.** Uno de los cuatro puntos de la rosa de los vientos (norte, este, sur y oeste) es _____ .

_____ **4.** Todos los mapas planos muestran alguna _____ , o representación errónea de la figura original.

_____ **5.** El globo terráqueo muestra los continentes de la Tierra en una menor _____ .

Columna II

a. escala

b. un punto cardinal

c. distorsión

d. una proyección

e. un globo terráqueo

B. Ideas principales

Instrucciones: En cada espacio en blanco, escribe la letra que mejor conteste la pregunta.

_____ **6.** Los mapas se inventaron, porque los globos terráqueos no pueden mostrar
    a. los nombres de los continentes.
    b. las formas de los continentes.
    c. suficiente detalle.
    d. la distancia entre los continentes.

_____ **7.** ¿Cuál es una desventaja de una proyección de Mercator?
    a. No incluye todos los continentes.
    b. No muestra detalles suficientes de la superficie terrestre.
    c. Es muy grande y difícil de cargar.
    d. Muestra las verdaderas formas pero no los verdaderos tamaños.

_____ **8.** ¿Por qué muchos geógrafos prefieren la proyección de Robinson?
    a. Muestra de manera exacta la forma y el tamaño de la mayoría del planeta.
    b. No tiene distorsión de la superficie de la Tierra.
    c. Es una proyección interrumpida y más exacta de la superficie terrestre.
    d. Es un mapa de áreas iguales.

_____ **9.** Para hallar los puntos cardinales en un mapa, debes referirte a
    a. los signos convencionales.
    b. la escala.
    c. la rosa de los vientos.
    d. la cuadrícula.

_____ **10.** Para hallar el símbolo que se usa para representar una carretera en un mapa, debes referirte a
    a. los signos convencionales.
    b. la escala.
    c. la rosa de los vientos.
    d. la cuadrícula.

El mundo de la geografía

Pregunta guía:

- ¿Cómo es la geografía de la Tierra?

La geografía es el estudio de la Tierra. Los geógrafos son guiados por dos preguntas básicas en su trabajo: (1) ¿Dónde están ubicadas las cosas? y (2) ¿Por qué están allí? Para hallar las respuestas, los geógrafos usan cinco temas para organizar la información. Esos temas son: la ubicación (dónde existe ese lugar en particular), el lugar (las características físicas y humanas del sitio), la interacción de los seres humanos con el medio ambiente (cómo afectan las personas su medio ambiente), los desplazamientos (cómo las personas, los productos y las ideas van de un lugar a otro) y las regiones (grandes zonas que están unidas por características semejantes).

Los geógrafos usan herramientas especiales para estudiar la superficie de la Tierra. Estas incluyen globos terráqueos y diferentes tipos de mapas. Los globos terráqueos ofrecen la representación más exacta de la Tierra. Desafortunadamente, son demasiado grandes para transportar fácilmente y demasiado pequeños para mostrar en más detalle. Los mapas planos son más fáciles de transportar y pueden ser muy detallados, pero tienen sus propios problemas. No se puede mostrar de manera exacta la redondez de la Tierra en una superficie plana, sin obtener alguna distorsión o representación errónea de la forma o del tamaño. La proyección de Mercator, es un mapa plano que los navegantes han usado por más de 400 años. Este representa formas correctas de las grandes masas pero no de los tamaños y de las distancias. Hoy en día muchos geógrafos prefieren la proyección de Robinson, que muestra tamaños, formas y distancias casi exactas, aunque se distorsiona en los bordes.

La mayoría de los mapas tienen partes especiales, como la rosa de los vientos, la escala, los signos convencionales y la cuadrícula. La rosa de los vientos muestra los puntos cardinales: norte, sur, este y oeste. La escala de los mapas nos indica qué distancia en la tierra representa cierta distancia en el mapa. Por ejemplo, en algunos mapas una pulgada puede representar una milla. En otros mapas, una pulgada puede equivaler a 100 millas. Los signos convencionales o inscripciones, explican los símbolos que representan aspectos como las carreteras y las ciudades. La cuadrícula del mapa le ayuda a las personas a hallar cosas en el mapa. Algunos mapas usan cuadrículas de paralelos y meridianos, otros usan cuadrículas de letras y números.

ACTIVIDAD DE VOCABULARIO

CAPÍTULO 1

El mundo de la geografía

Instrucciones: La lista de palabras a continuación contiene términos importantes del Capítulo 1. En otra hoja, escribe el significado de cada término. Si es necesario, observa cómo se usan los términos en el Capítulo 1.

1. **punto cardinal**—uno de los cuatro puntos de un compás: norte, sur, este y oeste

2. **rosa de los vientos**—figura que comúnmente aparece en los mapas y muestra los cuatro puntos cardinales

3. **grado**—unidad de medición usada para determinar una ubicación absoluta

4. **distorsión**—en los mapas, una deformación de una figura original

5. **línea ecuatorial**—línea imaginaria que rodea el globo terrestre por su zona más ancha

6. **geografía**—el estudio de la superficie terrestre, las conexiones entre los lugares, y las relaciones entre las personas y su medio ambiente

7. **globo terráqueo**—modelo redondo del planeta

8. **signos convencionales**—sección de un mapa que explica sus símbolos

9. **líneas de latitud**—serie de líneas imaginarias que rodean a la Tierra formando círculos paralelos a la línea ecuatorial; también llamadas paralelos

10. **líneas de longitud**—serie de líneas imaginarias que van del Polo Norte al Polo Sur; también llamadas meridianos

11. **meridiano**—línea imaginaria del globo terráqueo que se extiende del Polo Norte al Polo Sur

12. **paralelo**—cualquiera de las líneas imaginarias paralelas a la línea ecuatorial que rodean la tierra; una línea de latitud

13. **llanura**—región plana o de poco relieve

14. **Meridiano de Greenwich**—línea imaginaria de longitud, o meridiano, que va del Polo Norte al Polo Sur a través de Greenwich, Inglaterra

15. **proyección**—representación de la superficie redonda de la Tierra sobre una hoja plana de papel

16. **escala**—tamaño o proporción de algo en un mapa en comparación con su tamaño real

La geografía física de la Tierra

CAPÍTULO
2

La Línea Abierta de Ciencias Sociales

Querida familia:

En nuestra clase de ciencias sociales, seguimos la exploración de la geografía de nuestro planeta. Durante los próximos días, estudiaremos la geografía física del planeta. Exploraremos los movimientos de la Tierra en el espacio, las características físicas tanto del exterior como del interior de la superficie de la Tierra, y los climas del planeta. A medida que su hijo o hija aprende sobre la geografía física de la Tierra, usted puede señalar elementos geográficos significativos dentro de su comunidad o sus alrededores.

Los alumnos trabajarán en proyectos especiales para profundizar en su conocimiento de la geografía. Ellos pueden escoger entre varios proyectos que se describen en el libro de texto. Los proyectos incluyen: la creación de un juego de cartas de geografía, la preparación de una cartelera para exponer artículos de geografía que provengan de periódicos y revistas, la creación de un mapa detallado de una región o país en particular y la elaboración de una carpeta de presentación de un país determinado.

Usted puede ayudar mucho con esos proyectos. Si su hijo o hija está haciendo un juego de cartas de geografía, ofrezca su ayuda para ensayar el juego a medida que él o ella lo prepara. Si su hijo o hija está buscando artículos de geografía en periódicos y revistas, ayúdele a conseguir revistas interesantes e informativas que él o ella pueda usar para el proyecto. Si su hijo o hija está preparando una carpeta para la presentación del país de alguno de sus antepasados, sugiérale los nombres de los familiares qué él o ella podría entrevistar para el proyecto.

Espero que tanto usted como su hijo o hija disfruten el estudio de los diversos temas que conforman la geografía de nuestro planeta.

Atentamente,

Spanish Support

Nombre _____ Clase _____ Fecha _____

CAPÍTULO 2
**La geografía física
de la Tierra**

Nuestro planeta: La Tierra

A. Durante la lectura

Instrucciones: A medida que vayas leyendo la Sección 1, escribe tus respuestas a las siguientes preguntas en los espacios en blanco.

1. ¿Por qué llamamos a nuestra galaxia la Vía Láctea?

_____

2. ¿Por qué los días son más largos que las noches durante cierta época del año?

_____

3. ¿Cuándo ocurre el solsticio de verano en el Hemisferio Norte?

_____

4. ¿Por qué casi siempre hace calor en las zonas tropicales?

_____

B. Repaso de los términos clave

Instrucciones: Para completar cada oración, escribe el término correspondiente en el espacio en blanco.

5. La línea imaginaria que va a través de la Tierra desde el Polo Norte hasta el Polo Sur se llama

_____ .

6. Las zonas polares también se llaman latitudes _____ .

7. Las zonas templadas o de latitudes _____ tienen distintas estaciones durante el año.

8. El trayecto de forma ovalada que la tierra sigue alrededor del sol se llama _____ .

9. Mientras la Tierra gira alrededor del sol, también gira sobre su eje haciendo una

_____ completa cada 24 horas.

10. Cada año la Tierra completa una _____ alrededor del sol.

11. Casi siempre hace calor en los trópicos, o latitudes _____ .

CAPÍTULO 2
La geografía física
de la Tierra

Nuestro planeta: La Tierra

A. Términos y conceptos clave

Instrucciones: Empareja las definiciones de la Columna I con los términos de la Columna II.
Escribe la letra correspondiente en cada espacio en blanco.

Columna I

_____ 1. las regiones entre el Trópico de Cáncer y el Círculo Polar Ártico, y el Trópico de Capricornio y el Círculo Polar Antártico

_____ 2. una órbita completa de la Tierra alrededor del sol

_____ 3. el movimiento giratorio de la Tierra sobre sí misma

_____ 4. el trayecto que la Tierra sigue al girar alrededor del sol

_____ 5. la región entre el Trópico de Cáncer y el Trópico de Capricornio

Columna II

a. rotación

b. latitudes bajas

c. órbita

d. revolución

e. latitudes medias

B. Ideas principales

Instrucciones: En cada espacio en blanco, escribe la letra que mejor conteste la pregunta.

_____ 6. A medida que la Tierra gira en el espacio, en el lado que está frente al sol siempre es
   a. de noche.
   b. de día.
   c. invierno.
   d. verano.

_____ 7. ¿Qué factores causan los cambios en la temperatura durante las estaciones?
   a. las latitudes medias y altas
   b. la órbita de la Tierra y la línea ecuatorial
   c. la inclinación de la Tierra y su órbita
   d. la longitud de la Tierra y el Trópico de Cáncer

_____ 8. El clima en las zonas polares es muy frío, porque ellos
   a. sólo reciben luz directa del sol.
   b. reciben tanto luz directa como luz indirecta.
   c. no reciben luz directa del sol.
   d. no recibe nada de sol.

_____ 9. ¿Cuáles son las consecuencias de que el sol esté directamente sobre la línea ecuatorial el 21 de marzo y el 23 de septiembre?
   a. Los días y las noches no tienen la misma duración.
   b. Es de día durante casi 20 horas.
   c. Es de noche durante casi 20 horas.
   d. Los días y las noches tienen casi exactamente la misma duración.

_____ 10. El sol brilla directamente sobre el Trópico de Cáncer en el Hemisferio Norte en el
   a. solsticio de verano.
   b. solsticio de invierno.
   c. equinoccio de primavera.
   d. equinoccio de otoño.

© Prentice-Hall, Inc.

Spanish Support

Nombre _____ Clase _____ Fecha _____

LECTURA DIRIGIDA Y REPASO

CAPÍTULO 2
La geografía física
de la Tierra

Tierra, mar y aire

A. Durante la lectura

Instrucciones: A medida que vayas leyendo la Sección 2, completa la tabla a continuación con información de los continentes. Bajo cada idea principal, escribe dos ideas que la apoyen.

Idea principal A
Los geógrafos soportan la teoría de que hace millones de años sólo existía en la Tierra una gran masa de tierra llamada Pangea.
1. _____
2. _____
Idea principal B
Los continentes son parte de las placas en la corteza terrestre, que a lo largo del tiempo se han movido y deslizado en distintas direcciones.
3. _____
4. _____

B. Repaso de los términos clave

Instrucciones: Para completar cada oración, escribe el término correspondiente en el espacio en blanco.

5. Un accidente geográfico que es ancho en la base, que tiene una altura de más de 2,000 pies (610 m) y cuya cima termina en punta se llama _____ . Un accidente geográfico que es menos pendiente y cuya cima es redonda se llama _____ .

6. Una zona plana o de poco relieve se llama _____ .

7. Una zona plana que se eleva por encima del terreno a su alrededor se llama _____ .

8. Una forma o un tipo de terreno, como por ejemplo una montaña o un cerro se llama

_____ .

9. Cada gran sección de la corteza terrestre se llama _____ .

10. La idea de que la corteza terrestre está dividida en grandes placas es la teoría de

_____ .

CAPÍTULO 2
La geografía física
de la Tierra

Tierra, mar y aire

A. Términos y conceptos clave

Instrucciones: Lee las oraciones a continuación. Si una oración es verdadera, escribe V en el espacio en blanco. Si es falsa, escribe F. En otra hoja de papel, vuelve a escribir las oraciones falsas para convertirlas en verdaderas.

_____ **1.** Las extensas zonas planas o de poco relieve se llaman llanuras.

_____ **2.** Según la teoría de las placas tectónicas, la corteza terrestre está formada de una sola sección o placa.

_____ **3.** La partidura de rocas con maquinaria de construcción se conoce como desgaste climático.

_____ **4.** La franja de gases que rodea la Tierra se llama atmósfera.

_____ **5.** Las montañas y los cerros son ejemplos de accidentes geográficos.

B. Ideas principales

Instrucciones: En cada espacio en blanco, escribe la letra que mejor conteste la pregunta.

_____ **6.** ¿Qué accidente geográfico que se eleva a más de 2,000 pies (609.57 m) sobre el nivel del mar?
    a. una placa   **c.** una montaña
    b. un cerro   **d.** un valle

_____ **7.** Hace doscientos millones de años, toda la tierra del planeta
    a. estaba cubierta de agua.   **c.** estaba cubierta de bosques.
    b. formaba parte de una gran masa.   **d.** era parte del "Círculo de Fuego".

_____ **8.** ¿Cuáles son las tres causas del desgaste climático?
    a. el viento, la lluvia y el hielo
    b. los terremotos, los volcanes y la lluvia
    c. la erosión, el magma y el calor extremo
    d. las mareas, los terremotos y el frío extremo

_____ **9.** La atmósfera que rodea la Tierra da oxígeno que provee vida a
    a. las rocas.   **c.** las personas y los animales.
    b. las plantas.   **d.** los peces en el océano.

_____ **10.** El desgaste climático y la erosión transforman las rocas, y poco a poco forman
    a. oxígeno para las plantas.   **c.** las placas tectónicas.
    b. los polos de la Tierra.   **d.** nuevos accidentes geográficos.

Spanish Support

El proceso del clima

A. Durante la lectura

Instrucciones: A medida que vayas leyendo la Sección 3, completa los siguientes enunciados.

1. El clima de una zona es el promedio del _____ durante muchos años.

2. Los ríos rápidos que se mueven en el océano se llaman _____ , y ocurren a causa de la rotación de la Tierra.

3. En el verano, el clima de un pueblo cerca de un lago o del océano por lo general será más

   _____ que un zona que se encuentre alejada del agua.

4. Así como el viento y el agua pueden crear climas más suaves, también pueden causar

   _____ .

5. Los vientos violentos y los tormentas que se forman en los trópicos en el Océano Atlántico se llaman

   _____ . Las tormentas similares que se forman en el Océano Pacífico se llaman

   _____ .

6. Los tornados son embudos de remolinos y torbellinos de _____ que algunas veces pueden alcanzar una velocidad de 200 millas (322 kilómetros) por hora.

B. Repaso de los términos clave

Instrucciones: En el espacio en blanco a continuación, escribe la definición de los siguientes términos clave.

7. el estado del tiempo

   _____

8. la temperatura

   _____

9. la precipitación

   _____

10. el clima

   _____

CAPÍTULO 2
La geografía física de la Tierra

El proceso del clima

A. Términos y conceptos clave

Instrucciones: Empareja las definiciones de la Columna I con los términos de la Columna II.
Escribe la letra correspondiente en cada espacio en blanco.

Columna I

_____ 1. En la India, las personas tienen razones muy serias para observar ____ o los cambios diarios del viento.

_____ 2. El nivel de calor o frío de algo, como del aire o del agua, se llama ____ .

_____ 3. Una corriente del Océano Atlántico que va hacia el norte y el este de los trópicos se llama ____ .

_____ 4. El agua que cae sobre la tierra en forma de lluvia, granizo, aguanieve o nieve se llama ____ .

_____ 5. La corriente que viaja al norte desde la Antártica hasta la costa de Sur América es ____ .

Columna II

a. la temperatura

b. la precipitación

c. la corriente del Perú

d. el estado del tiempo

e. la Corriente del Golfo

B. Ideas principales

Instrucciones: En cada espacio en blanco, escribe la letra que mejor conteste la pregunta.

_____ 6. El patrón ambiental que se da en una zona durante un largo período de tiempo es
  a. la precipitación.
  b. el estado del tiempo.
  c. el clima.
  d. la temperatura.

_____ 7. ¿Qué le sucedería a la Tierra si no tuviera viento y agua?
  a. Se volvería muy fría.
  b. Se volvería muy caliente.
  c. No rotaría de manera uniforme.
  d. No estaría en órbita con el sol.

_____ 8. ¿Por qué la temperatura siempre está más fresca cerca del agua en un caluroso día de verano?
  a. El agua cubre la mayor parte de la superficie terrestre.
  b. Las corrientes recorren grandes distancias.
  c. El agua tarda más que la tierra en calentarse o enfriarse.
  d. El agua caliente se desplaza hacia el norte.

_____ 9. Las tormentas son importantes para las personas porque
  a. transportan agua fresca.
  b. vuelven los climas más suaves.
  c. siempre causan mareas.
  d. ayudan a enfriar la tierra.

_____ 10. Tanto las corrientes de aire como las del océano son formadas por
  a. la rotación de la Tierra.
  b. la revolución de la Tierra.
  c. el aire caliente que se eleva.
  d. las altas montañas.

Spanish Support

Nombre _____ Clase _____ Fecha _____

LECTURA DIRIGIDA Y REPASO

CAPÍTULO 2
La geografía física
de la Tierra

4 El efecto del clima en la vegetación

A. Durante la lectura

Instrucciones: A medida que vayas leyendo la Sección 4, completa la siguiente tabla con información detallada de los climas tropicales, moderados y polares.

Vegetación y clima

	Clima tropical	Clima moderado	Clima polar
Ubicación	1.	2.	3.
Vegetación	4.	5.	6.
Estaciones	7.	8.	9.

B. Repaso de los términos clave

Instrucciones: En el espacio en blanco a continuación, escribe la definición de los siguientes términos clave.

10. vegetación

_____

11. bóveda de follaje

_____

12. tundra

_____

13. clima vertical

_____

CAPÍTULO 2
La geografía física
de la Tierra

El efecto del clima en la vegetación

A. Términos y conceptos clave

Instrucciones: Empareja las definiciones de la Columna I con los términos de la Columna II.
Escribe la letra correspondiente en cada espacio en blanco.

Columna I

_____ 1. capa de ramas y hojas en la copa de los árboles en un bosque

_____ 2. región fría en la que sólo pueden crecer ciertas plantas, como los pastos de crecimiento lento

_____ 3. los patrones climáticos de una región, considerados con base en su elevación

_____ 4. las plantas de una región o zona

_____ 5. la región de los Estados Unidos donde crecen altos pastos

Columna II

a. la tundra

b. la vegetación

c. la Gran Llanura

d. el clima vertical

e. la bóveda de follaje

B. Ideas principales

Instrucciones: En cada espacio en blanco, escribe la letra que mejor conteste la pregunta.

_____ 6. ¿Qué necesitan las plantas para sobrevivir en un clima en particular?
   a. raíces, agua y vientos
   b. enredaderas, alimento y lluvia
   c. agua, luz solar y ciertas sustancias nutritivas
   d. vegetación, adaptaciones y luz solar

_____ 7. Los geógrafos hablan de cinco tipos de climas: tropical, seco, moderado, continental y
   a. bosque húmedo.   c. desértico.
   b. polar.   d. océanico.

_____ 8. Como los climas áridos y semiáridos reciben poca lluvia, las plantas crecen
   a. con raíces profundas.
   b. muy alejadas unas de otras en suelos arenosos.
   c. con hojas grandes y carnosas.
   d. muy juntas unas de otras en suelos fértiles.

_____ 9. Como las temperaturas en los climas moderados casi nunca están por debajo del nivel de congelación, la vegetación en esas zonas
   a. se limita a pastos solamente.   c. se limita a arbustos solamente.
   b. se limita a árboles solamente.   d. es muy variada.

_____ 10. ¿Por qué no hay vegetación en la cima del Monte Everest?
   a. Es demasiado frío para que sobreviva cualquier tipo de planta.
   b. No hay oxígeno ni dióxido de carbono a esa altura.
   c. Es demasiado húmedo para que las plantas puedan sobrevivir.
   d. La luz del sol es demasiado fuerte para las plantas.

Spanish Support

RESUMEN DEL CAPÍTULO

CAPÍTULO
2

La geografía física de la Tierra

Pregunta guía:

- ¿Cómo es la geografía de la Tierra?

La geografía física de la Tierra incluye: la superficie terrestre, el aire, el agua, el clima y la vegetación. El movimiento de la Tierra a través del espacio afecta todas esas características. La Tierra rota una vez al día sobre su eje inclinado y eso causa que ocurran el día y la noche. A medida que la Tierra completa su órbita alrededor del sol una vez al año, la inclinación de su eje causa cambios en la duración del día y la noche, así como en la temperatura. Esos cambios de temperatura causan las estaciones.

Los científicos creen que hace 200 millones de años, toda la tierra del planeta era parte de un sólo supercontinente conocido como Pangea. A lo largo de millones de años Pangea se dividió y formó los continentes separados que hoy conocemos. Los científicos usan la teoría de las placas tectónicas para explicar por qué se dividió Pangea. Grandes masas de tierra, o placas tectónicas, flotan lentamente en el magma que está bajo ellas, modificando la forma de la superficie de la Tierra. El movimiento de las placas, cuando rozan unas con otras, puede causar terremotos y volcanes.

El desgaste climático y la erosión son dos fuerzas que poco a poco transforman los accidentes geográficos de la superficie de la Tierra. Durante ese proceso de transformación, la erosión lleva el material que desplaza a distintos lugares donde se forman nuevos accidentes geográficos. El viento, la lluvia y la nieve forman parte de esos procesos.

La Tierra está rodeada de una gruesa capa de gases especiales que llamamos la atmósfera. La atmósfera mantiene el calor del planeta y provee oxígeno y dióxido de carbono para los animales y las plantas.

El estado del tiempo consiste en los cambios que se dan día a día en la temperatura del aire y la precipitación. El clima es el promedio del estado del tiempo durante muchos años en una región en particular. El clima depende de la latitud y del movimiento de las corrientes del aire y del océano. Los geógrafos han identificado cinco tipos generales de clima: tropical, seco, moderado, continental y polar. Cada uno cuenta con vegetación, temperatura, cantidad de lluvia y estaciones únicas.

La geografía física de la Tierra

Instrucciones: Empareja las definiciones de la Columna I con los términos de la Columna II. Escribe la letra correspondiente en cada espacio en blanco. Si es necesario, busca los términos en el glosario de tu libro de texto.

Columna I

_____ 1. una órbita completa de la Tierra alrededor del sol

_____ 2. el movimiento giratorio de la Tierra

_____ 3. formación geológica con una cima redonda y de menor inclinación que una montaña

_____ 4. el trayecto de la Tierra alrededor del sol

_____ 5. las plantas de una zona

_____ 6. la región entre el Trópico de Cáncer y el Trópico de Capricornio

_____ 7. una zona extensa, por lo general plana, que se eleva por encima del terreno a su alrededor

_____ 8. las regiones entre el Círculo Polar Ártico y el Polo Norte, y el Círculo Polar Antártico y el Polo Sur

_____ 9. en geografía, una gran sección de la corteza terrestre

_____ 10. agua que cae sobre la tierra desde la atmósfera

_____ 11. una formación geológica que se eleva, por lo general, a más de 2,000 pies sobre el nivel del mar

_____ 12. la franja de gases que rodea la Tierra

_____ 13. extensa región plana o de poco relieve

_____ 14. los patrones ambientales que se dan en una zona a lo largo del tiempo

_____ 15. el grado de calor o frío que puede tener una sustancia química

_____ 16. condición de la capa inferior de la atmósfera terrestre, en un lugar específico durante un breve período de tiempo

Columna II

a. atmósfera

b. clima

c. latitudes altas

d. cerro

e. latitudes bajas

f. montaña

g. órbita

h. llanura

i. placa

j. meseta

k. precipitación

l. revolución

m. rotación

n. temperatura

o. vegetación

p. tiempo

Spanish Support

CARTAS PARA LA FAMILIA

La geografía humana de la Tierra

La Línea Abierta de Ciencias Sociales

Querida familia:

Durante los próximos días, en nuestra clase de ciencias sociales exploraremos la geografía humana de la Tierra. Aprenderemos en dónde vive la mayor parte de la población, por qué viven en esos lugares, cómo está creciendo la población y por qué migran las personas. Si usted sabe alguna historia personal o de la familia sobre migración, le puede servir como un buen vehículo para discutir algunos de los temas de este capítulo.

Cuando pasee por su vecindario o comunidad, observe con su hijo o hija la densidad de la población. Hable de los factores que pueden haber influido en ello. Los factores pueden incluir: el clima, los accidentes geográficos, o la facilidad de acceso a los ríos, lagos o mares. Anime a su hijo o hija a que estime la densidad de la población en donde viven (el número total de personas, dividido entre el número total de millas cuadradas o kilómetros cuadrados).

Busque artículos o informes en las noticias sobre el crecimiento de la población y las dificultades que está creando en distintas partes del mundo. Esa puede ser una buena manera de empezar una conversación sobre el material del Capítulo 3. Los artículos pueden incluir temas como: la escasez de alimentos, ciudades con exceso de población, falta de empleo y las migraciones. Si tiene acceso al *Internet,* usted y su hijo o hija pueden buscar información sobre población y migración en muchas partes del mundo.

Durante las próximas semanas, le enviaremos más información sobre las culturas y los recursos naturales de nuestro planeta. Espero que se diviertan mientras comparte el maravilloso mundo de la geografía con su hijo o hija.

Atentamente,

CAPÍTULO 3

La geografía humana de la Tierra

¿Dónde viven las personas?

A. Durante la lectura

Instrucciones: A medida que vayas leyendo la Sección 1, escribe tus respuestas a las siguientes preguntas en los espacios en blanco.

1. ¿Cuáles son las tres cosas que investigan los demógrafos para entender la distribución de la población?

_____

2. ¿Qué porcentaje de la Tierra está cubierta por los océanos?

_____

3. ¿Qué regiones son las más difíciles para la sobrevivencia humana?

_____

4. ¿Bajo qué tipo de características geográficas empezaron la mayoría de las grandes civilizaciones?

_____

5. ¿Por qué tan pocas familias fueron a vivir a la Gran Llanura de los Estados Unidos en un principio?

_____

6. ¿Cómo se las arreglan algunas personas para vivir comodamente en climas con calor o frío extremo?

_____

B. Repaso de los términos clave

Instrucciones: Escribe las definiciones de los siguientes términos clave, en los espacios en blanco a continuación.

7. población

_____

8. distribución de la población

_____

9. demógrafo

_____

10. densidad de la población

_____

Spanish Support

EXAMEN DE LA SECCIÓN

¿Dónde viven las personas?

A. Términos y conceptos clave

Instrucciones: Lee las oraciones a continuación. Si una oración es verdadera, escribe V en el espacio en blanco. Si es falsa, escribe F. En otra hoja de papel, vuelve a escribir las oraciones falsas para convertirlas en verdaderas.

_____ **1.** Un demógrafo estudia la geografía de la Tierra.

_____ **2.** La manera en que la población está esparcida en una región se llama la distribución de la población.

_____ **3.** La densidad de población es el número total de personas que vive en una región en particular.

_____ **4.** La población mundial es el número total de personas que viven en el planeta.

_____ **5.** El valle del Río Nilo tiene una de las densidades de población más bajas del mundo.

B. Ideas principales

Instrucciones: En cada espacio en blanco, escribe la letra que mejor conteste la pregunta.

_____ **6.** ¿En cuál de las siguientes zonas esperarías que vivieran muchas personas?
  a. en una zona montañosa
  b. en una zona plana cerca a un río
  c. en un desierto árido y caluroso
  d. en el Océano Pacífico

_____ **7.** ¿Cuál de las siguientes características te puede indicar que un continente podría tener una densidad de población baja?
  a. tierra fértil
  b. bastos recursos naturales
  c. pocos ríos y poca lluvia
  d. buen clima

_____ **8.** Para hallar la densidad de la población de un lugar, divide el número de habitantes entre el número de
  a. montañas.
  b. ríos.
  c. millas cuadradas o kilómetros cuadrados.
  d. países.

_____ **9.** En un mapa de la población mundial, las zonas cercanas al agua tienen
  a. una densidad de población mayor.
  b. una distribución de población menor.
  c. una población promedio.
  d. una densidad de población menor.

_____ **10.** Para sobrevivir en los áridos desiertos, las personas han desarrollado
  a. tuberías para transportar agua de otros lugares.
  b. tecnologías avanzadas para crear agua de la arena.
  c. la habilidad de sobrevivir sin beber agua.
  d. estilos de vida que se adaptan al ambiente del desierto.

CAPÍTULO 3
La geografía
humana de la
Tierra

Una población en crecimiento

A. Durante la lectura

Instrucciones: A medida que vayas leyendo la Sección 2, completa la siguiente tabla con información del crecimiento de la población.

Causas y efectos del crecimiento de la población

Causas	Efectos
Hace cien años, en los Estados Unidos, el índice de mortalidad era más alto, las provisiones de alimento más escasas y muchos morían por enfermedades.	1.
El índice de natalidad ha aumentado rápidamente y el índice de mortalidad ha disminuido.	2.
Nuevas medicinas y nuevos tipos de cirugía combaten los problemas de la salud y las enfermedades.	3.
4.	Algunas naciones del suroeste asiático enfrentan escasez de agua potable y energía.
5.	La destrucción de los bosques de la India y Pakistán afectan la fuente de aire puro del planeta.

B. Repaso de los términos clave

Instrucciones: Para completar cada oración, escribe el término correspondiente en el espacio en blanco.

6. El número de años promedio que se espera que viva una mujer en los Estados Unidos, conocido

 también como _____ , es de 80 años.

7. Los cambios en los métodos de cultivo que ocurrieron durante la década de los sesenta se conoce

 como _____ .

8. El número de nacimientos anuales por cada 1,000 habitantes se conoce como _____ .

9. Cuando el índice de natalidad es más alto que el de _____ , significa que la
 población está creciendo.

Spanish Support

EXAMEN DE LA SECCIÓN

Una población en crecimiento

A. Términos y conceptos clave

Instrucciones: Empareja las definiciones de la Columna I con los términos de la Columna II.
Escribe la letra correspondiente en cada espacio en blanco.

Columna I

_____ **1.** el número de muertes registradas anualmente por cada 1,000 habitantes

_____ **2.** los cambios en la agricultura a partir de los años cincuenta, que han aumentado de manera considerable la reserva mundial de alimentos

_____ **3.** el tiempo que se espera que una persona viva

_____ **4.** el número de nacimientos anuales por cada 1,000 habitantes

_____ **5.** una medicina que se usa para combatir algunas enfermedades

Columna II

a. la revolución verde

b. el índice de mortalidad

c. el promedio de vida

d. la vacuna

e. el índice de natalidad

B. Ideas principales

Instrucciones: En cada espacio en blanco, escribe la letra que mejor conteste la pregunta.

_____ **6.** En tiempos modernos, la población mundial
  a. ha disminuido.
  b. ha crecido bastante.
  c. ha crecido poco.
  d. no ha cambiado.

_____ **7.** Los demógrafos pueden averiguar el crecimiento de la población mundial al comparar
  a. el promedio de vida de los hombres y las mujeres.
  b. las enfermedades que hay en el mundo.
  c. los índices de mortalidad y de natalidad.
  d. las reservas de alimento del mundo.

_____ **8.** ¿Cómo han afectado a la población mundial los avances científicos en medicina y los cambios en métodos de agricultura?
  a. Las personas viven más años que antes.
  b. Nacen más bebés con problemas graves de salud.
  c. El índice de mortalidad ha aumentado.
  d. El índice de natalidad ha disminuido.

_____ **9.** Las poblaciones estables usan recursos de manera más lenta que las poblaciones que
  a. viven en los Estados Unidos.
  b. viven Europa.
  c. están disminuyendo.
  d. están aumentando.

_____ **10.** ¿Qué efecto negativo causa en el medio ambiente el crecimiento acelerado de la población?
  a. un menor número de trabajos para un mayor número de personas
  b. se necesita un mayor número de árboles para mantener los terrenos en su lugar
  c. la disminución de los bosques de la India
  d. el mantenimiento de corrientes de agua fresca

CAPÍTULO 3

La geografía humana de la Tierra

¿Por qué migran las personas?

A. Durante la lectura

Instrucciones: A medida que vayas leyendo la Sección 3, completa la siguiente tabla con información de la migración de las personas. Bajo cada idea principal, escribe dos ideas que la apoyen.

Idea principal A
La teoría de "empuje y atracción" explica muchas de las tendencias migratorias en la historia.

I. _____

_____

2. _____

_____

Idea principal B
Aunque muchas personas dejan su país de origen para vivir en otro país, las migraciones también pueden ocurrir dentro de un mismo país.

3. _____

_____

4. _____

_____

B. Repaso de los términos clave

Instrucciones: En el espacio en blanco a continuación, escribe la definición de los siguientes términos clave.

5. La idea de que ciertas razones (que por lo general son económicas) obligan a las personas a mudarse de un país a otro, se conoce como _____ .

6. Una persona que _____ , o se muda de un lugar a otro se llama

_____ .

7. A una ciudad también se le conoce como una zona _____ . A una aldea o zona menos poblada también se le conoce como una zona _____ .

8. Muchas personas se mudan de pueblos pequeños a las ciudades. Ese proceso se llama

_____ .

Spanish Support

¿Por qué migran las personas?

A. Términos y conceptos clave

Instrucciones: Empareja las definiciones de la Columna I con los términos de la Columna II.
Escribe la letra correspondiente en cada espacio en blanco.

Columna I

_____ **1.** una persona que se muda a otro país con la intención de residir allí

_____ **2.** una región con una densidad de población baja, como el campo

_____ **3.** el desplazamiento de personas de un país o región a otro

_____ **4.** el desplazamiento de personas a las ciudades

_____ **5.** una zona con una alta densidad de población, como una ciudad

Columna II

a. migración

b. zona urbana

c. urbanización

d. zona rural

e. inmigrante

B. Ideas principales

Instrucciones: En cada espacio en blanco, escribe la letra que mejor conteste la pregunta.

_____ **6.** ¿Cuál de las siguientes opciones es una razón económica por la cual las personas emigran?
   a. No les gusta la forma de gobierno.   **c.** Huyen de una guerra.
   b. No consiguen trabajo.   **d.** Son perseguidos por su religión.

_____ **7.** ¿Para qué usan los demógrafos la teoría de "empuje y atracción"?
   a. para explicar cambios climáticos   **c.** para describir cambios políticos
   b. para explicar la inmigración   **d.** para describir cambios geográficos

_____ **8.** En las décadas de 1840 y 1850, muchas personas salieron de Irlanda hacia los Estados Unidos, porque
   a. se estaban muriendo de hambre.   **c.** buscaban mejores trabajos.
   b. estaban huyendo de una guerra.   **d.** querían vivir en ciudades grandes.

_____ **9.** Recientemente, las personas en los Estados Unidos se han mudado a los estados del sur y suroeste en busca de
   a. mejores sistemas de transporte.   **c.** mejores trabajos y mejores climas.
   b. mejores escuelas.   **d.** libertad para practicar su religión.

_____ **10.** Debido al crecimiento acelerado de la población, Sao Pablo, Brasil, no le puede dar a sus habitantes suficientes
   a. viviendas y trabajos.   **c.** televisores.
   b. automóviles.   **d.** radios.

La geografía humana de la Tierra

Pregunta guía:

- ¿Dónde viven las personas de la Tierra?

La mayoría de los habitantes en el mundo vive en regiones cercanas al agua, con tierras fértiles y un clima moderado con lluvias adecuadas. Los continentes más poblados son Asia, Europa y América del Norte. Las personas tienden a vivir en lugares donde puedan mantener intercambio comercial, cultivar productos y usar los recursos naturales. Los otros continentes (América del Sur, África y Australia) tienen poblaciones menores porque es más difícil vivir allí. A pesar de que en esos continentes hay algunas zonas que son excelentes para vivir, también tienen desiertos áridos, montañas altas y bosques densos en los cuales no pueden vivir muchas personas.

Durante el siglo XX, el índice de natalidad ha crecido mientras que el índice de mortalidad ha disminuido. El resultado es un crecimiento acelerado de la población, debido a una reserva de alimentos mayor y a los avances de la medicina. En algunos países, la población se duplica en menos de 20 años. Las personas hoy viven más tiempo que antes. Hace cien años, las personas en los Estados Unidos por lo general vivían menos de 50 años. Hoy en día, el promedio de vida aproximado para una mujer es de 80 años y para un hombre es de 73 años.

Por siglos, las personas se han mudado de sus lugares de origen. A eso lo llamamos migración. Los inmigrantes son personas que dejan un país para vivir en otro. Los demógrafos, que son científicos que estudian la población humana, usan la teoría de "empuje y atracción" para explicar la migración. La teoría dice que las personas que emigran son "empujadas" de su tierra natal debido a situaciones económicas desfavorables o a condiciones políticas adversas. Dichas personas son "atraídas" por la esperanza de una mejor vida en otro lugar. En muchos lugares, más y más personas se mudan de las zonas rurales a las zonas urbanas por razones económicas, y causan así el crecimiento de las ciudades, también conocido como urbanización.

Spanish Support

ACTIVIDAD DE VOCABULARIO

La geografía humana de la Tierra

Instrucciones: Las palabras subrayadas en las oraciones a continuación son términos clave importantes del Capítulo 3. En la parte de atrás de esta hoja o en otra hoja de papel, escribe tus propias oraciones con los términos o con otras versiones de los términos. Si es necesario, busca los términos en el glosario de tu libro de texto.

1. La población mundial pasará de 3 billones a 6.4 billones entre el año de 1960 y el año 2000.

2. La distribución de la población describe cómo se ha esparcido la población por la Tierra.

3. Un demógrafo examina los índices de natalidad, de matrimonios y de mortalidad para saber más acerca de la población mundial.

4. La densidad de la población varía mucho de un lugar a otro.

5. El índice de natalidad en los Estados Unidos ha aumentado por muchos años.

6. Los demógrafos pueden calcular el crecimiento de la población al comparar el índice de natalidad y el índice de mortalidad.

7. Por muchos siglos, el promedio de vida de la persona promedio era bajo.

8. La revolución verde ha aumentado enormemente la reserva mundial de alimentos.

9. Cuando las personas se mudan de un lugar a otro, se llama migración.

10. Muchos inmigrantes irlandeses fueron a vivir a las ciudades del noreste de los Estados Unidos durante las décadas de 1840 y 1850.

11. La teoría de "empuje y atracción" es una teoría con la que los demógrafos explican la migración.

12. La urbanización es una tendencia común en muchas partes del mundo.

13. Una zona rural tiene una densidad de población baja.

14. La ciudad de Nueva York es una zona urbana.

CAPÍTULO
4

Las culturas del mundo

La Línea Abierta de Ciencias Sociales

Querida familia:

Para continuar con nuestros estudios de la geografía de la Tierra, vamos a estudiar las culturas del mundo. Su hijo o hija aprenderá acerca de las diferencias y similitudes que hay entre las distintas culturas del mundo. Para explorar las características de las culturas, observaremos los grupos sociales, los lenguajes y los sistemas políticos y económicos de diferentes culturas. También aprenderemos la manera en que cambian las diferentes culturas y nos concentraremos en cómo hoy en día la mayoría de las culturas del mundo están cambiando rápidamente.

Simplemente con hablar de las distintas maneras en que las familias hacen las cosas, ayudará a su hijo o hija a prepararse para cubrir el material del Capítulo 4. Usted podría hablarle a él o ella sobre las experiencias de su infancia o las de sus padres o abuelos, para comparar las estructuras de la familia en el pasado con las de hoy en día. Esos ejemplos pueden ilustrar los cambios que han ocurrido en su propia vida. También podrían explorar juntos las experiencias de los hijos de sus amigos y familiares.

Podemos ver cambios culturales a todo nuestro alrededor. Cada día surgen nuevas ideas, nueva terminología y nuevas tecnologías. La música nos llega de todas partes del mundo. Por ejemplo, observe cómo cambia la cultura en la música, los empleos, los medios de comunicación, los deportes y las ciencias. Para buscar buenos ejemplos, podría asistir con su hijo o hija a una feria de ciencias o a un museo de tecnología.

Espero que tanto usted como su hijo o hija sigan disfrutando al compartir estas exploraciones de la Tierra y su geografía.

Atentamente,

Spanish Support

LECTURA DIRIGIDA Y REPASO

¿Qué es la cultura?

A. Durante la lectura

Instrucciones: A medida que vayas leyendo la Sección 1, completa los siguientes enunciados.

1. Los geógrafos usan niveles de tecnología para ver qué tan _____ es una cultura.

2. En Bali, Indonesia, los habitantes cortan las montañas en forma de _____ para crear terrenos aptos para el cultivo.

3. Antes de la revolución agraria, nuestros antepasados dependían de _____ para obtener casi todos sus alimentos.

4. Cuando nuestros antepasados aprendieron a crear y a usar el fuego, algunos de ellos empezaron a vivir en zonas más _____ .

5. Una cultura se convierte en una civilización cuando sus habitantes crean un sistema de _____ para registrar su conocimiento y transmitirlo a los demás.

B. Repaso de los términos clave

Instrucciones: En el espacio en blanco a continuación, escribe la definición de los siguientes términos clave.

6. cultura

_____

7. rasgo cultural

_____

8. tecnología

_____

9. paisaje cultural

_____

10. agricultura

_____

EXAMEN DE LA SECCIÓN

CAPÍTULO 4
**Las culturas
del mundo**

¿Qué es la cultura?

A. Términos y conceptos clave

Instrucciones: Lee las oraciones a continuación. Si una oración es verdadera, escribe V en el espacio en blanco. Si es falsa, escribe F. En otra hoja de papel, vuelve a escribir las oraciones falsas para convertirlas en verdaderas.

_____ **1.** La cultura es la forma de vida de un grupo de personas que comparte determinadas costumbres y creencias.

_____ **2.** El paisaje cultural de un grupo incluye todos los cambios de su medio ambiente.

_____ **3.** Las destrezas particulares, las costumbres y las maneras de hacer las cosas de un grupo determinado se denominan características individuales.

_____ **4.** La tecnología se refiere a las herramientas de trabajo y a las destrezas que las personas necesitan para usarlas.

_____ **5.** La agricultura fue un elemento importante en el desarrollo de las primeras culturas.

B. Ideas principales

Instrucciones: En cada espacio en blanco, escribe la letra que mejor conteste la pregunta.

_____ **6.** ¿Cuál de los siguientes enunciados acerca de las culturas es cierto?
   a. La cultura incluye el trabajo de las personas, su comportamiento y sus creencias.
   b. Con frecuencia, la cultura cambia rápidamente.
   c. La cultura no incluye las cosas materiales
   d. El idioma no es parte de la cultura

_____ **7.** ¿Cuál de los siguientes enunciados podría estudiar un geógrafo para saber cómo afectan los accidentes geográficos la cultura de una zona?
   a. la manera en que los deportes afectan el idioma
   b. la manera en que las montañas afectan la agricultura
   c. la manera en que la televisión afecta a las familias
   d. la manera en que el *Internet* afecta la literatura

_____ **8.** ¿En qué medio ambiente estarían los granjeros más dispuestos a formar terrazas para sus cultivos?
   a. en el valle ancho y plano de un río
   b. en la cima de una meseta
   c. en las montañas
   d. en las llanuras bajas y planas

_____ **9.** ¿Por cuántos estados dicen los geógrafos que tienen que pasar las primeras culturas?
   a. dos
   b. tres
   c. cuatro
   d. cinco

_____ **10.** Una cultura que crea un sistema de escritura es
   a. una sociedad tecnológica.
   b. una cultura tradicional.
   c. una sociedad agrícola.
   d. una civilización.

Spanish Support

LECTURA DIRIGIDA Y REPASO

Grupos sociales, idioma y religión

A. Durante la lectura

Instrucciones: A medida que vayas leyendo la Sección 2, completa la siguiente tabla con información de los continentes. Bajo cada idea principal, escribe dos ideas que la apoyen.

Idea principal A
Toda cultura tiene su propia estructura social, es decir, un sistema de grupos pequeños dentro de grupos más grandes.
I. _____
2. _____

Idea principal B
Toda cultura tiene como base el idioma.
3. _____
4. _____

B. Repaso de los términos clave

Instrucciones: En el espacio en blanco a continuación, escribe la definición de los siguientes términos clave.

5. estructura social _____

6. familia nuclear _____
_____

7. familia extensa _____

8. ética _____
_____

Nombre _____ Clase _____ Fecha _____

CAPÍTULO 4
Las culturas del mundo

Grupos sociales, idioma y religión

A. Términos y conceptos clave

Instrucciones: Empareja las definiciones de la Columna I con los términos de la Columna II. Escribe la letra correspondiente en cada espacio en blanco.

Columna I

_____ 1. La unidad familiar que incluye la madre, el padre y los hijos es _____ .

_____ 2. Toda cultura tiene _____ , es decir, una manera de organizar a las personas en grupos más pequeños.

_____ 3. Muchas culturas tienen familias _____ , en las que los hombres toman la mayoría de las decisiones.

_____ 4. Las religiones guían a las personas en su _____ , o estándares de comportamineto moral.

_____ 5. Muchas veces, varias generaciones viven juntas en _____ .

Columna II

a. una familia extensa

b. patriarcales

c. ética

d. una familia nuclear

e. una estructura social

B. Ideas principales

Instrucciones: En cada espacio en blanco, escribe la letra que mejor conteste la pregunta.

_____ 6. La unidad social más importante de una cultura es
a. la escuela.
b. el gobierno.
c. la familia.
d. el ejército.

_____ 7. Muchas culturas tienen familias matriarcales donde
a. el padre es el que manda.
b. la madre es la que manda.
c. los abuelos son los que mandan.
d. los profesores son los que mandan.

_____ 8. La organización social es importante para una cultura, porque ayuda a que las personas
a. aprendan literatura.
b. viajen a otros lugares.
c. aprendan acerca de la geología del lugar.
d. trabajen juntas para satisfacer sus necesidades básicas.

_____ 9. ¿Cuáles son tres elementos importantes de una cultura?
a. los alimentos, el vestido y el intercambio comercial
b. el lenguaje, los valores morales y la religión
c. los valores morales, la geología y la biología
d. la literatura, la geografía y el intercambio comercial

_____ 10. ¿Cuál de los siguientes enunciados es cierto acerca del lenguaje?
a. El lenguaje ayuda a las personas a transmitir sus conocimientos y creencias a sus hijos.
b. Las personas usan el mismo lenguaje en todos los países del mundo.
c. El lenguaje no puede mostrar lo que es importante para las personas.
d. El lenguaje de un país nunca cambia.

Spanish Support

Los sistemas económicos y políticos

A. Durante la lectura

Instrucciones: A medida que vayas leyendo la Sección 3, completa la siguiente tabla con detalles de los tres sistemas económicos principales.

Los sistemas económicos

	Capitalismo	Socialismo	Communismo
¿Quiénes son los dueños de los negocios?	1.	2.	3.
¿Quiénes deciden cuánto pagarle a los trabajadores y cómo hacer uso de las ganancias?	4.	5.	6.

B. Repaso de los términos clave

Instrucciones: Para completar cada oración, escribe el término correspondiente en el espacio en blanco.

7. Cuando un rey o una reina están encargados del gobierno, el sistema se llama _____ .

8. Un sistema que organiza las leyes de la sociedad y las hace cumplir se llama _____ .

9. Una persona que recibe un bien o servicio es _____ .

10. En los primeros sistemas de gobierno, las personas vivían en grupos pequeños y llevaban a cabo los asuntos diarios del grupo. Eso se llama _____ .

11. Los tres sistemas de gobierno principales son _____ , _____ , y _____ .

12. Una persona que tiene casi todo el control de un país es _____ .

13. Cuando los ciudadanos eligen representantes para que gobiernen el país, se llama

_____ .

Nombre _____ Clase _____ Fecha _____

CAPÍTULO 4
Las culturas
del mundo

Los sistemas económicos y políticos

3

A. Términos y conceptos clave

Instrucciones: Empareja las definiciones de la Columna I con los términos de la Columna II. Escribe la letra correspondiente en cada espacio en blanco.

Columna I

_____ 1. un sistema en el que las personas y las compañías privadas son dueñas de empresas de productos básicos y no básicos

_____ 2. un gobernante que tiene todo el control de un país

_____ 3. un gobierno en el que las personas participan de manera directa en la toma de decisiones

_____ 4. una persona que compra bienes y servicios

_____ 5. un sistema diseñado para producir, distribuir, consumir y establecer la propiedad de bienes, servicios y la riqueza

Columna II

a. democracia directa

b. capitalismo

c. dictador

d. economía

e. consumidor

B. Ideas principales

Instrucciones: En cada espacio en blanco, escribe la letra que mejor conteste la pregunta.

_____ 6. ¿Cuáles son los dos tipos de productos de toda economía?
  a. computadores y automóviles
  b. bienes y servicios
  c. agricultura y tecnología
  d. negocios y tecnología

_____ 7. Un negocio básico en un sistema económico podría producir
  a. equipos para hacer ejercicio.
  b. discos compactos.
  c. autobuses.
  d. zapatos de atletismo.

_____ 8. ¿Cuáles son los tres sistemas económicos principales?
  a. el comunismo, la democracia y el capitalismo
  b. el socialismo, la monarquía absoluta y la dictadura
  c. el comunismo, el capitalismo y el socialismo
  d. el consumismo, el capitalismo y la monarquía

_____ 9. El sistema que establece y hace cumplir las leyes de la sociedad y las instituciones se llama
  a. una monarquía.
  b. un gobierno.
  c. una economía.
  d. una tecnología.

_____ 10. En una democracia representativa, los ciudadanos eligen representantes que
  a. establecen una monarquía.
  b. establecen el idioma de la cultura.
  c. dictan las leyes.
  d. crean nuevas tecnologías.

Spanish Support

El cambio cultural

A. Durante la lectura

Instrucciones: A medida que vayas leyendo la Sección 4, escribe tus respuestas a las siguientes preguntas en los espacios en blanco.

1. ¿Qué cosas pueden afectar la cultura?

_____

2. ¿Cómo puede explicar la difusión cultural la historia de los "jeans"?

_____

3. ¿Cuál es un ejemplo contemporáneo de la aculturación en los deportes?

_____

4. ¿Cómo ha acelerado el proceso de cambio cultural la nueva tecnología?

_____

5. ¿Por qué algunas personas se refieren a la Tierra como a "un pueblo global"?

_____

6. ¿Cómo han cambiado las culturas en relación con su medio ambiente?

_____

B. Repaso de los términos clave

Instrucciones: En el espacio en blanco a continuación, escribe la definición de los siguientes términos clave.

7. difusión cultural

_____

8. aculturación

_____

CAPÍTULO 4
Las culturas
del mundo

El cambio cultural

A. Términos y conceptos clave

Instrucciones: Lee las oraciones a continuación. Si una oración es verdadera, escribe V en el espacio en blanco. Si es falsa, escribe F. En otra hoja de papel vuelve a escribir las oraciones falsas para hacerlas verdaderas.

_____ **1.** La transmisión de costumbres de una cultura a otra se llama cambio cultural.

_____ **2.** La aculturación es el proceso de tomar prestadas rutas comerciales entre las culturas.

_____ **3.** Hoy en día, muchas personas llaman a la Tierra "un pueblo global".

_____ **4.** Las ideas nuevas pueden cambiar a una cultura.

_____ **5.** Si una cultura cambia muy lentamente, sus habitantes se pueden confundir y la cultura puede llegar a peligrar.

B. Ideas principales

Instrucciones: En cada espacio en blanco, escribe la letra que mejor conteste la pregunta.

_____ **6.** Un cambio en el clima de un lugar puede cambiar una cultura al afectar
    a. la aculturación.   **c.** su historia pasada.
    b. los alimentos que las personas cultivan.   **d.** el pueblo global.

_____ **7.** La preocupación mundial por el medio ambiente, que comenzó en la década de años cincuenta, es un ejemplo de
    a. exceso de información.   **c.** cambios culturales.
    b. cambios en el medio ambiente.   **d.** cambios tecnológicos.

_____ **8.** Enviar una nave espacial en órbita es un ejemplo de cómo
    a. la tecnología cambia nuestra cultura.   **c.** el clima cambia nuestra cultura.
    b. las costumbres cambian nuestra cultura.   **d.** la geología cambia nuestra cultura.

_____ **9.** Como resultado de los últimos avances tecnológicos, el cambio cultural
    a. ha disminuido.   **c.** no ha afectado a nadie.
    b. ha afectado a muy pocas personas.   **d.** ha acelerado.

_____ **10.** ¿Por qué hay personas que trabajan para salvar sus propias culturas?
    a. para desarrollar nuevos inventos
    b. para evitar que se pierdan las tradiciones más valiosas
    c. para salvar su medio ambiente
    d. para proteger los avances tecnológicos

Spanish Support

RESUMEN DEL CAPÍTULO

Las culturas del mundo

Pregunta guía:

- ¿Qué es la cultura?

La cultura es la forma de vida de un grupo de personas que comparten costumbres, creencias e ideas similares. Los geógrafos quieren saber cómo los accidentes geográficos, el clima, la vegetación y los recursos afectan la cultura. Esos efectos son parte del tema de la interacción de los seres humanos con el medio ambiente.

Las primeras culturas se desarrollaron a través de largos períodos de tiempo. Los geógrafos dividen el desarrollo de las primeras culturas en los siguientes estados: la invención de las herramientas, el descubrimiento del fuego, el desarrollo de la agricultura y el uso de la escritura.

Toda cultura tiene una estructura social, es decir, una manera de organizar a las personas en grupos pequeños con tareas particulares. La familia es la unidad social más importante de cualquier cultura. Los niños aprenden de sus familias las costumbres y tradiciones de su cultura. En algunas culturas, la unidad familiar básica es la familia nuclear: es decir, la madre, el padre y los hijos. En otras culturas, la unidad básica es la familia extensa, que incluye miembros de varias generaciones que viven en el mismo lugar. El lenguaje es otra parte importante de la cultura. Permite que las personas comuniquen lo que necesitan compartir dentro de su cultura.

Existen varios tipos de sistemas económicos. Los principales son el capitalismo, el socialismo y el comunismo. También existen distintos tipos de sistemas políticos que incluyen: la democracia directa, la democracia representativa, la monarquía y la dictadura. En cada sistema, el control de los bienes, servicios, riqueza y poder está dividido de alguna manera entre el gobierno y los ciudadanos.

Muchos factores, tales como ideas nuevas, la tecnología y la emigración pueden causar cambios culturales. En los últimos años, los cambios culturales han ocurrido más y más rápido. Un cambio importante es el que ha ocurrido en las comunicaciones modernas, en el que personas particulares, empresas y el gobierno se pueden comunicar de manera casi instantánea de cualquier lugar a cualquier otro lugar cercano o lejano. Sin embargo, los cambios tan rápidos pueden ser destructivos. Por lo general, la tecnología moderna reemplaza las antiguas fuentes de conocimiento, las cuales se pueden perder para siempre. Muchas personas trabajan hoy en día para preservar los elementos importantes de sus culturas.

Las culturas del mundo

Instrucciones: Empareja las definiciones de la Columna I con los términos de la Columna II. Escribe la letra correspondiente en cada espacio en blanco. Si es necesario, busca los términos en el glosario de tu libro de texto.

Columna I

_____ 1. un sistema de gobierno en el que las personas participan de manera directa en la toma de decisiones

_____ 2. un sistema de gobierno en el que gobierna un rey o una reina

_____ 3. un conjunto de leyes que define el poder del gobierno

_____ 4. el trabajo que se hace para otras personas, como el trabajo que lleva a cabo un doctor

_____ 5. cultivar

_____ 6. el sistema que establece y hace que se cumplan las leyes de una sociedad y sus instituciones

_____ 7. la manera en que las personas dentro de una cultura, están organizadas en grupos más pequeños

_____ 8. sistema de gobierno en el que las personas eligen representantes para que manejen los asuntos de su país

_____ 9. productos hechos para la venta, como los automóviles

_____ 10. característica del comportamiento de las personas, tal como el idioma, que pasa de una generación a otra

_____ 11. un sistema para producir, distribuir, consumir y establecer la propiedad de bienes, servicios y riqueza

_____ 12. un paisaje que ha sido alterado por un grupo de personas y que refleja su cultura

_____ 13. un sistema económico en el que el gobierno es dueño de todas las empresas e industrias

_____ 14. la forma de vida de las personas que comparten creencias similares

_____ 15. un sistema económico en el que individuos y compañías privadas son dueños de la mayoría de las empresas e industrias de productos básicos y no básicos

Columna II

a. agricultura

b. capitalismo

c. comunismo

d. constitución

e. paisaje cultural

f. rasgo cultural

g. cultura

h. democracia directa

i. economía

j. bienes

k. gobierno

l. monarquía

m. democracia representativa

n. servicios

o. estructura social

Spanish Support

CARTAS PARA LA FAMILIA

Recursos naturales de la Tierra

La Línea Abierta de Ciencias Sociales

Querida familia:

A medida que nuestra clase de ciencias sociales completa su estudio de la geografía del mundo, exploraremos los recursos naturales de la Tierra y sus usos. Aprenderemos cómo las personas afectan el medio ambiente. Como vimos en el Capítulo 4, el rápido crecimiento de la población está ejerciendo gran presión en los recursos naturales mundiales. Para empezar una conversación al respecto con su hijo o hija, puede hablar de la importancia de reciclar y de usar productos reciclados.

En una sección del Capítulo 5 aprenderemos más sobre los recursos naturales renovables, tales como los árboles y los cultivos, y los recursos naturales no renovables, tales como el petróleo y los minerales. Cuando escuche o vea las noticias con su hijo o hija, pueden hablar acerca de las noticias que traten sobre distintos tipos de recursos. Si hace poco tiempo estuvo de viaje o si maneja por su vecindario, puede hablar de cómo usan la tierra allí. ¿Vive usted en una zona rural y agrícola? ¿Vive usted en una zona urbana, donde la tierra está cubierta con estructuras?

Un vistazo alrededor de su casa puede servir para iniciar una conversación con su hijo o hija sobre la actividad económica. ¿De dónde vienen los productos que hay en su casa? ¿Hay alguno de ellos que sea el resultado directo de su trabajo, como un pez que haya pescado o un objeto que usted mismo haya construido? ¿Hay productos hechos por alguien que usted conozca en su comunidad? ¿Cuáles productos vienen de otros lugares a través de algún distribuidor?

Anime a su hijo o hija a recortar artículos de noticias sobre la polución y los efectos que causa en el medio ambiente. También podría hablarle de los lugares donde usted ha observado polución en el aire, la tierra o en las extensiones de agua dentro y alrededor de su comunidad.

Espero que hayan disfrutado este tema de la geografía de la Tierra. Apreciamos mucho su ayuda a medida que trabajamos juntos con su hijo o hija.

Atentamente,

CAPÍTULO 5
Recursos naturales de la Tierra

¿Qué son los recursos naturales?

A. Durante la lectura

Instrucciones: A medida que vayas leyendo la Sección 1, completa la siguiente tabla a continuación con información de los recursos naturales.

Recurso original

Recurso original	Tipo de recurso	Usos posibles
Árbol	1.	2.
Maíz	3.	4.
Agua	5.	6.
Gas natural	7.	8.

B. Repaso de los términos clave

Instrucciones: Escribe las definiciones de los siguientes términos clave, en los espacios en blanco a continuación.

9. recurso natural

_____

10. recurso reciclable

_____

11. materia prima

_____

12. recurso renovable

_____

13. recurso no renovable

_____

14. combustible fósil

_____

Spanish Support

EXAMEN DE LA SECCIÓN

¿Qué son los recursos naturales?

A. Términos y conceptos clave

Instrucciones: Completa los espacios en blanco de la Columna I con los términos de la Columna II. Escribe la letra correspondiente en cada espacio en blanco.

Columna I

_____ **1.** Un recurso en su estado natural es ____ .

_____ **2.** Cualquier material útil que hallemos en el medio ambiente es ____ .

_____ **3.** Cuando ____ , como el petróleo, se usa del todo, no puede ser reemplazado.

_____ **4.** Un material que puede ser reemplazado después ser usado se llama ____ .

_____ **5.** Un material que pasa por ciclos de procesos naturales en el medio ambiente es ____ .

Columna II

a. materia prima

b. un recurso reciclable

c. un recurso no renovable

d. un recurso natural

e. un recurso renovable

B. Ideas principales

Instrucciones: En cada espacio en blanco, escribe la letra que mejor conteste la pregunta.

_____ **6.** Cualquier cosa proveniente del planeta que sirva para satisfacer las necesidades de alimento, vestido o vivienda de las personas es
   a. un accidente geográfico.
   b. una cultura.
   c. un recurso.
   d. un fósil.

_____ **7.** Los geógrafos llaman al agua
   a. un recurso no renovable.
   b. un recurso reciclable.
   c. materia prima.
   d. un recurso sintético.

_____ **8.** ¿Cuál de los siguientes enunciados es un ejemplo del uso indirecto de energía?
   a. un reloj que funciona con electricidad
   b. un automóvil que usa gasolina
   c. una escoba de fábrica
   d. un horno que usa gas natural

_____ **9.** Durante millones de años, los restos de las plantas y los animales prehistóricos han creado
   a. recursos renovables.
   b. recursos reciclables.
   c. combustibles sintéticos.
   d. combustibles fósiles.

_____ **10.** ¿Cuál de los siguientes enunciados sobre los recursos energéticos del planeta es verdadero?
   a. Todos los países tienen las mismas cantidades de petróleo, carbón y gas natural.
   b. Los recursos energéticos no están esparcidos por igual en el mundo.
   c. No es necesario hallar más fuentes de energía.
   d. En 1973, los países del Medio Oriente decidieron vender más petróleo.

CAPÍTULO 5
Recursos naturales de la Tierra

El uso de los terrenos

A. Durante la lectura

Instrucciones: A medida que vayas leyendo la Sección 2, escribe tus respuestas a las siguientes preguntas en los espacios en blanco.

1. ¿En que nivel de actividad económica se convierte la materia prima en productos útiles?

   _____

2. ¿Qué sucedió durante la revolución industrial?

   _____

3. ¿Qué tipos de cosas pueden detener el traslado de bienes y servicios de un país a otro?

   _____

4. ¿Cuáles son algunos de los retos que tienen que enfrentar las naciones en vía de desarrollo?

   _____

B. Repaso de los términos clave

Instrucciones: Para completar cada oración, escribe el término correspondiente en el espacio en blanco.

5. La agricultura realizada en grandes granjas, que son propiedad de empresas en lugar de familias

   pequeñas, se llama _____ .

6. Por lo general, los gobiernos de los países desarrollados ofrecen préstamos, o _____ ,
   a los gobiernos de los países en vía de desarrollo.

7. Cuando los agricultores sólo cultivan alimento suficiente para alimentar a su familia, practican lo que

   se conoce como _____ .

8. Una granja comercial que emplea a muchos trabajadores, pero que pertenece a pocas personas

   se llama _____ .

9. Un país que tiene poca industria es un país _____ , mientras que un país con mucha

   industria es un país _____ .

10. El proceso de convertir materia prima en un producto terminado se conoce como

    _____ .

Spanish Support

EXAMEN DE LA SECCIÓN

El uso de los terrenos

A. Términos y conceptos clave

Instrucciones: Empareja las definiciones de la Columna I con los términos de la Columna II. Escribe la letra correspondiente en cada espacio en blanco.

Columna I

_____ **I.** una sociedad industrial moderna

_____ **2.** agricultura realizada por empresas

_____ **3.** el proceso de convertir materia prima en un producto terminado

_____ **4.** una finca grande en la que se cultiva un solo producto para la exportación

_____ **5.** ayuda económica y militar a otro país

Columna II

a. manufactura

b. plantación

c. ayuda extranjera

d. agricultura industrial

e. nación desarrollada

B. Ideas principales

Instrucciones: En cada espacio en blanco, escribe la letra que mejor conteste la pregunta.

_____ **6.** Convertir materia prima en productos que la gente pueda usar es
   a. el primer nivel de desarrollo económico.
   b. el segundo nivel de desarrollo económico.
   c. el tercer nivel de desarrollo económico.
   d. el cuarto nivel de desarrollo económico.

_____ **7.** ¿Cuál de los siguientes enunciados es un ejemplo de primer nivel de actividad económica?
   a. la manufactura   **c.** la ganadería
   b. la distribución   **d.** el procesamiento

_____ **8.** La revolución industrial separó a los países del mundo en
   a. los países del norte y los países del sur.
   b. los países desarrollados y los países en vía de desarrollo.
   c. los países del este y los países del oeste.
   d. los países antiguos y los países modernos.

_____ **9.** Muchas personas en los países desarrollados obtienen su alimento de
   a. la agricultura de subsistencia.   **c.** las plantaciones.
   b. la agricultura comercial.   **d.** la agricultura de desarrollo.

_____ **10.** La mayoría de las personas del mundo viven en
   a. América del Norte y América del Sur.   **c.** los países desarrollados.
   b. los Estados Unidos.   **d.** los países en vía de desarrollo.

CAPÍTULO 5
Recursos naturales de la Tierra

El efecto que tenemos en el medio ambiente

A. Durante la lectura

Instrucciones: A medida que vayas leyendo la Sección 3, completa la siguiente tabla con información de las personas y el medio ambiente. Bajo cada idea principal, escribe dos ideas que la apoyen.

Idea principal A
Los seres vivientes están ligados a sus ecosistemas y ciertos cambios pueden destruir esos ecosistemas.

1. _____

_____

2. _____

_____

Idea principal B
Muchos países y organizaciones están haciendo esfuerzos para reducir el uso de productos que son nocivos para el medio ambiente.

3. _____

_____

4. _____

_____

B. Repaso de los términos clave

Instrucciones: Para completar cada oración, escribe el término correspondiente en el espacio en blanco.

5. Una manera de evitar la desaparición de las especies en vía de extinción es defender el medio ambiente en el que viven, o su _____ .

6. Una capa de gas en la superficie de la atmósfera, conocida como _____ , bloquea la mayor parte de los nocivos rayos ultravioleta emitidos por el sol.

7. La mayoría de los gobiernos de las ciudades en Estados Unidos animan a las personas a volver a usar, o a _____ , muchos materiales usados, como periódicos, botellas y latas.

8. Cuando los productos químicos se mezclan con el vapor del agua en el aire, se forman

_____ .

9. La liberación al aire de gases al aire del llamado "de invernadero" puede ser la causa del

_____ .

© Prentice-Hall, Inc.

Spanish Support

EXAMEN DE LA SECCIÓN

El efecto que tenemos en el medio ambiente

CAPÍTULO 5
Recursos naturales de la Tierra

A. Términos y conceptos clave

Instrucciones: Lee las oraciones a continuación. Si una oración es verdadera, escribe V en el espacio en blanco. Si es falsa, escribe F. Vuelve a escribir las oraciones falsas para convertirlas en verdaderas.

I. Una comunidad de seres vivientes y su medio ambiente se llama hábitat.

_____

2. La capa de ozono es una capa gaseosa en la superficie de la atmósfera.

_____

3. Reciclar significa usar sólo materiales nuevos para formar nuevos productos.

_____

4. El proceso de arrasar los árboles para despejar el terreno se llama forestación.

_____

5. El calentamiento del planeta consiste en un aumento pequeño en la temperatura de la Tierra a causa del aumento en la cantidad de dióxido de carbono en la atmósfera.

_____

B. Ideas principales

Instrucciones: En cada espacio en blanco, escribe la letra que mejor conteste la pregunta.

_____ **6.** ¿Cuál de las siguientes opciones es un ejemplo de un ecosistema?
  a. una especie en vía de extinción
  b. el valle del Río Amazonas
  c. el monumento a Washington
  d. una hoja de césped

_____ **7.** ¿Cuál es el objetivo del Acta para las Especies en Vía de Extinción (*Endangered Species Act*)?
  a. proteger accidentes geográficos importantes
  b. fomentar la creación de nuevas especies silvestres
  c. detener la extinción de plantas y animales
  d. aconsejar a las personas a volver a usar recursos naturales

_____ **8.** La causa de la lluvia ácida es el uso de
  a. combustibles fósiles.
  b. energía nuclear.
  c. envases de aerosol con atomizador.
  d. energía solar.

_____ **9.** ¿Cuál de las siguientes opciones es una fuente de energía alternativa a los combustibles fósiles?
  a. el carbón
  b. el gas natural
  c. el petróleo
  d. el viento

_____ **10.** En la década de los setenta, los científicos hallaron que los clorofluorocarbonos (CFCs) estaban destruyendo
  a. los bosques de Nueva York.
  b. la capa de ozono.
  c. el bosque tropical del Amazonas.
  d. las reservas de combustibles fósiles.

Los recursos naturales de la Tierra

Pregunta guía:

- ¿Cómo usamos los recursos del planeta?

<u>Los recursos naturales son materiales útiles que se hallan en el medio ambiente, como por ejemplo: el agua, los minerales, la tierra y la vegetación.</u> Los recursos naturales se usan para muchas cosas, incluyendo alimento, combustible, vestido y vivienda. Hay tres tipos de recursos. Los recursos reciclables (como el agua) tienen un ciclo natural en el medio ambiente. Los recursos renovables (como los árboles) se pueden reemplazar. Los recursos no renovables (como el petróleo y el carbón) no se pueden reemplazar una vez que se han usado.

<u>Los geógrafos han identificado tres niveles en el uso de los recursos.</u> En el primer nivel, se usan la tierra y los recursos directamente para hacer otros productos. Se caza, se corta leña, se excavan minas y se pesca. En el segundo nivel, se convierte la materia prima en productos terminados, por medio del proceso de fabricación o manufactura. En el tercer nivel, se ofrece un servicio en lugar de un producto. A ese nivel los productos no son distribuidos por las mismas personas que los fabrican.

<u>Hoy en día, los países del mundo se dividen en dos categorías principales: los países desarrollados y los países en vía de desarrollo.</u> Los países desarrollados tienen muchas industrias, mientras que los países en vía de desarrollo tienen pocas. La mayoría de los habitantes de los países desarrollados viven en pueblos o ciudades. Muchos habitantes de los países en vía de desarrollo viven en zonas rurales y sobreviven de la agricultura o de la cría de animales.

<u>Los ecosistemas son lugares en donde los seres vivientes y los elementos no vivientes que forman su medio ambiente dependen unos de otros para su sobrevivencia.</u> Los desiertos, los bosques húmedos y las llanuras son algunos ejemplos de ecosistemas. <u>Si una parte de un ecosistema cambia, las otras partes son afectadas.</u> Algunas actividades humanas, como la deforestación de los bosques húmedos en América del Sur, pueden destruir un ecosistema. La polución de las fábricas de automóviles puede causar lluvia ácida, destruir los ciclos del agua y destruir la capa de ozono. Para resolver esos problemas, los científicos están en la búsqueda de fuentes de energía que causen menos polución. Investigan nuevos usos de la energía nuclear, del viento y de la energía solar.

ACTIVIDAD DE VOCABULARIO

Los recursos naturales de la Tierra

Instrucciones: Las palabras subrayadas en las oraciones a continuación son términos clave del Capítulo 5. En la parte de atrás de esta hoja o en otra hoja de papel, escribe tus propias oraciones con los términos o con otras versiones de los términos. Si es necesario, busca los términos en el glosario de tu libro de texto.

1. **recurso natural**—todo material útil del medio ambiente que los seres humanos usan para sobrevivir

2. **materia prima**—recurso que aún se encuentra en su estado natural

3. **recurso reciclable**—recurso que pasa por los ciclos naturales del medio ambiente

4. **recurso renovable**—recurso natural que el medio ambiente sigue reemplazando a medida que es usado

5. **recurso no renovable**—recurso natural que no se puede reemplazar una vez que se ha usado

6. **combustible fósil**—recurso formado por los restos de plantas y animales

7. **manufactura**—el proceso de convertir materia prima en un producto terminado

8. **país desarrollado**—sociedad industrial moderna con una economía avanzada

9. **país en vía de desarrollo**—país con una producción industrial relativamente baja

10. **agricultura industrial**—agricultura realizada por compañías industriales

11. **agricultura de subsistencia**—agricultura que sólo provee suficiente alimento para mantener a una familia o a un pueblo

12. **plantación**—gran extensión de terreno donde el trabajo lo realizan trabajadores que viven en el lugar

13. **ayuda extranjera**—ayuda económica y militar que un país brinda a otro

14. **ecosistema**—una comunidad de seres vivientes y su medio ambiente

15. **deforestación**—el proceso de arrasar los árboles o los bosques para despejar el terreno

16. **hábitat**—el medio ambiente natural en el que una planta o animal vive y se desarrolla

17. **lluvia ácida**—lluvia con un alto contenido de sustancias químicas que contamina el medio ambiente

18. **capa de ozono**—capa de gas en la superficie de la atmósfera que bloquea la mayor parte de los nocivos rayos ultravioleta del sol

19. **calentamiento del planeta**—pequeño aumento en la temperatura de la Tierra

20. **reciclar**—volver a usar materiales para fabricar nuevos productos

Glosario

A

acculturation
aculturación el proceso de aceptación, asimilación e intercambio de ideas y características entre culturas

acid rain
lluvia ácida lluvia con un alto contenido de sustancias químicas que contamina y deteriora el medio ambiente; por lo general es causada por el uso excesivo de combustibles

agriculture
agricultura incluye el cultivo de la Tierra y la ganadería

atmosphere
atmósfera las capas de gas que rodean la Tierra

axis
eje línea imaginaria alrededor de la cual gira un planeta; la Tierra gira alrededor de un eje imaginario entre el Polo Norte y el Polo Sur

B

birthrate
índice de natalidad cifra anual de nacimientos por cada 1,000 personas

C

canopy
bóveda de follaje la capa más alta de las ramas y las hojas en un bosque

capitalism
capitalismo sistema económico en el que individuos y compañías privadas poseen y controlan la mayoría de empresas e industrias de productos básicos y no básicos

cardinal direction
punto cardinal uno de los cuatro puntos de un compás: norte, sur, este y oeste

climate
clima patrones ambientales típicos que se dan una zona durante un largo período de tiempo

commercial farming
agricultura industrial agricultura con tecnología moderna que compañías industriales llevan a cabo en grandes extensiones de tierra; también incluye la producción agrícola y la ganadería de exportación

communism
comunismo sistema económico en el que el gobierno posee y controla todas las empresas e industrias

compass rose
rosa de los vientos figura que comúnmente aparece en los mapas y muestra los cuatro puntos cardinales

Spanish Support

Glosario

constitution
constitución conjunto de leyes que define y limita el poder de un gobierno

consumer
consumidor persona que compra productos y servicios

culture
cultura forma de vida de un grupo de personas que comparte costumbres y creencias similares

cultural diffusion
difusión cultural la transmisión de costumbres e ideas de una cultura a otra

cultural landscape
paisaje cultural paisaje que ha sido alterado por los seres humanos y que refleja su cultura

cultural trait
rasgo cultural características de un grupo de personas, como su lenguaje, o una costumbre o una habilidad específica, que es transmitida de generación en generación

D

death rate
índice de mortalidad número anual de fallecimientos por cada 1,000 personas

deforestation
deforestación proceso de arrasar los árboles o la floresta de una zona, generalmente con el objeto de despejar terreno para la construcción de viviendas o para la agricultura

degree
grado unidad de medición usada para determinar una ubicación absoluta; la latitud y la longitud en los mapas se miden en grados

demographer
demógrafo científico que estudia las poblaciones humanas, incluyendo su tamaño, índice de crecimiento, densidad, distribución, e índices de nacimiento, matrimonios y mortalidad

developed nation
país desarrollado sociedad industrial moderna con una economía bien desarrollada

developing nation
país en vía de desarrollo país con producción industrial relativamente baja; por lo general, carente de tecnología moderna

dictator
dictador gobernante que ejerce poder absoluto sobre un país

direct democracy
democracia directa sistema de gobierno en el que la gente participa directamente en la toma de decisiones

distortion
distorsión deformación de una figura original; toda proyección para un mapa usada por un cartógrafo produce alguna distorsión

Glosario

E

economy
economía sistema de producción, distribución, propiedad y consumo de productos, servicios y riqueza

ecosystem
ecosistema una comunidad de seres vivientes y su medio ambiente; todos los elementos de un ecosistema interactúan mutuamente

Equator
línea ecuatorial línea imaginaria que rodea el globo terrestre por su zona más ancha (el punto medio entre el Polo Norte y el Polo Sur) y divide la Tierra en dos mitades llamadas hemisferios; la línea ecuatorial se usa como el punto de referencia para medir las latitudes norte y sur

erosion
erosión proceso mediante el cual el agua, el viento o el hielo arrastran pedazos de tierra a otro lugar

ethics
ética patrones de conducta moral que un individuo, una religión, un grupo, una profesión o una comunidad usa para distinguir entre el bien y el mal

extended family
familia extensa unidad familiar que puede incluir padres, hijos, hermanos, tíos, abuelos, bisabuelos y otros parientes

F

foreign aid
ayuda extranjera ayuda económica y militar que un país da a otro

fossil fuel
combustible fósil cualquier recurso mineral no renovable formado por los restos de plantas y animales; por ejemplo: el carbón, la gasolina y el gas natural

G

geography
geografía el estudio de la superficie terrestre, los procesos que la forman, las conexiones entre los lugares, y las relaciones entre las personas y su medio ambiente

global warming
calentamiento del planeta aumento en la temperatura de la Tierra debido a un incremento en la cantidad de dióxidos de carbono en la atmósfera; si hay demasiado dióxido de carbono en la atmósfera, ésta concentra el calor y hace que suba la temperatura del planeta

globe
globo terráqueo modelo redondo del planeta que muestra la verdadera forma de los continentes y los océanos

© Prentice-Hall, Inc.

Spanish Support

Recursos del Capítulo y la Sección ■ 51

Glosario

good
bienes productos hechos para la venta; los automóviles, las canastas, los computadores y el papel son ejemplos de bienes

government
gobierno sistema que establece las instituciones y las leyes en una sociedad y que se encarga de que estas últimas se cumplan; algunos gobiernos son controlados por pocas personas y otros por muchas personas

Green Revolution
la revolución verde cambios agrícolas que desde mediados de este siglo han logrado aumentar la producción mundial de alimentos; sin embargo, la revolución verde tiene un precio: la tecnología costosa y los pesticidas que utiliza pueden destruir el medio ambiente y las finanzas de un país

H

habitat
hábitat el medio ambiente natural en el que una planta o animal vive y se desarrolla

high latitudes
latitudes altas las regiones que se hallan entre el Círculo Polar Ártico y el Polo Norte, y entre el Círculo Polar Antártico y el Polo Sur

hill
cerro formación que se eleva más allá de la superficie del terreno a su alrededor y que tiene una cima redondeada; un cerro por lo general es más bajo y menos empinado que una montaña

I

immigrant
inmigrante persona que se muda a otro país con la intención de residir allí

K

key
signo convencional sección de un mapa que explica los símbolos que representan los fenómenos geográficos; también suele llamarse *inscripción*

L

landform
accidente geográfico forma de una zona de la superficie de la Tierra; las montañas y las colinas son ejemplos de accidentes geográficos

Glosario

latitude lines
líneas de latitud serie de líneas imaginarias, también llamadas paralelos, que rodean a la Tierra formando círculos paralelos a la línea ecuatorial; se usan para medir distancias en grados al norte o al sur de la línea ecuatorial

life expectancy
promedio de vida el promedio de años que se puede esperar que una persona viva

longitud lines
líneas de longitud serie de líneas imaginarias, también llamadas meridianos, que van del Polo Norte al Polo Sur; se usan para medir distancias en grados al este o al oeste del Meridiano de Greenwich

low latitudes
latitudes bajas las regiones entre el Trópico de Cáncer y el Trópico de Capricornio

M

manufacturing
manufactura proceso que transforma la materia prima en un producto terminado

meridian
meridiano línea imaginaria del globo terráqueo que se extiende del Polo Norte al Polo Sur; las líneas de longitud en los mapas o en los globos terráqueos son los meridianos

middle latitudes
latitudes medias las regiones comprendidas entre el Trópico de Cáncer y el Círculo Artico y el Trópico de Capricornio y el Círculo Antártico

migration
emigración cambio de personas de un país o región a otro con intención de residir en el nuevo lugar

monarchy
monarquía sistema de gobierno autoritario encabezado por un monarca, por lo general un rey o reina, instituido por derecho heredado

mountain
montaña formación geológica que se eleva a más de 2,000 pies de altura (610 m) por encima del nivel del mar y cuya base es más ancha que la cima

N

natural resource
recursos naturales cualquier materia obtenida del medio ambiente que se utiliza para subsistir y satisfacer necesidades básicas de la gente; algunos ejemplos de recursos naturales son: el agua, los minerales, el suelo y las plantas

Glosario

nonrenewable resource
recursos no renovables cualquier recurso natural que no se puede reemplazar una vez que se ha agotado; algunos recursos naturales no renovables son: combustibles fósiles como el carbón y el petróleo, y minerales como el hierro, el cobre y el oro

nuclear family
familia nuclear unidad familiar que incluye madre, padre e hijos

O

orbit
órbita trayecto seguido por un cuerpo celeste al girar alrededor de otro cuerpo; por ejemplo, la órbita de la tierra alrededor del sol

ozone layer
capa de ozono capa de gas en la superficie de la atmósfera que bloquea la mayor parte de los nocivos rayos ultravioleta emitidos por el sol

P

parallel
paralelo término geográfico que se refiere a cualquiera de las líneas imaginarias paralelas a la línea ecuatorial que rodean la tierra; una línea de latitud

plain
llanura región plana o de poco relieve, que por lo general se encuentra cerca de una costa

plantation
plantación gran extensión de terreno, por lo general en una zona cálida, donde generalmente se cultiva un solo producto para la exportación; el trabajo lo realizan trabajadores que viven en el lugar

plate
placa en términos geográficos, una enorme sección de la corteza terrestre

plateau
meseta zona plana extensa que se eleva por encima del terreno a su alrededor; por lo menos uno de sus costados es muy empinado

plate tectonics
placa tectónica teoría que sugiere que la corteza terrestre está compuesta de grandes planchas de roca llamadas placas, las cuales se desplazan lentamente

population
población personas que habitan en una región en particular; se refiere específicamente al número total de habitantes en una región

population density
densidad de población número promedio de personas que habitan en una región en particular

Glosario

population distribution
distribución de población manera en que la población está esparcida en una región

precipitation
precipitación el agua que cae sobre la tierra desde la atmósfera; como por ejemplo: la lluvia, el granizo y la nieve

Prime Meridian
Meridiano de Greenwich línea imaginaria de longitud, o meridiano, que va del Polo Norte al Polo Sur a través de Greenwich, Inglaterra; a esta línea se le ha designado 0° de longitud y se usa como punto de referencia, a partir del cual se miden las longitudes este y oeste

producer
fabricante persona o entidad que hace los productos que otras personas usan

projection
proyección representación de la superficie redonda de la Tierra sobre una hoja plana de papel

"push-pull" theory
teoría de "empuje y atracción" teoría de emigración que sostiene que la gente emigra porque ciertos aspectos de sus vidas les "empujan" a partir, y ciertos aspectos del nuevo lugar les "atraen"

R

raw material
materia prima recurso o materia que aún se encuentra en su estado natural y que todavía no ha sido procesado o convertido en un producto útil

recyclable resource
recurso reciclable recurso que pasa por los ciclos naturales del medio ambiente; el agua, el nitrógeno y el carbono son algunos de ellos

recycle
reciclar volver a usar materiales para fabricar nuevos productos

renewable resource
recurso renovable recurso natural que el medio sigue supliendo o reemplazando a medida que es usado; los árboles y las cosechas son recursos renovables

representative democracy
democracia representativa sistema de gobierno en el que las personas eligen representates para que manejen los asuntos del país

revolution
revolución en términos geográficos, una vuelta completa de la Tierra alrededor del sol; la Tierra completa una revolución alrededor del sol cada 365 1/4 días, o sea, cada año

rotation
rotación movimiento giratorio que la Tierra realiza alrededor de su propio eje (como un trompo), a medida que viaja por el espacio; a la Tierra le toma aproximadamente 24 horas hacer una rotación

Glosario

rural area
zona rural zona de baja densidad de población, tal como un pueblo o un campo

S

scale
escala tamaño o proporción de un mapa en comparación con la región que representa

services
servicios trabajo o deberes que una persona realiza para otras; por ejemplo: el trabajo de un médico o el de una persona que arregla televisores

socialism
socialismo sistema económico en que el gobierno es propietario de la mayoría de las industrias básicas, como los bancos y los sistemas de transporte y de comunicación; las industrias que no son básicas pertenecen a compañías privadas

social structure
estructura social la manera en que las personas dentro de una cultura, están organizadas en grupos más pequeños; cada grupo pequeño tiene sus propias funciones

subsistence farming
agricultura de subsistencia práctica que sólo provee suficiente comida y animales para mantener a una familia o a un pueblo

T

technology
tecnología herramientas de trabajo y destrezas necesarias para usarlas adecuadamente

temperature
temperatura el grado de calor o de frío que puede tener algo, como, por ejemplo, el agua o el aire; la temperatura se puede medir con un termómetro

tundra
tundra región cuya temperatura es siempre fría y en la cual solamente pueden crecer unas pocas plantas, como ciertos pastos de crecimiento lento

U

urban area
zona urbana zona con gran densidad de población, como una ciudad

urbanization
urbanización aumento de población en las ciudades causado por la inmigración de gente

V

vegetation
vegetación las plantas de una zona en particular

Glosario

vertical climate
clima vertical patrones climáticos de una región, considerados con base en la elevación de la zona; mientras mayor sea la elevación, más frío será el clima

W

weather
tiempo condición de la capa inferior de la atmósfera terrestre, en un lugar específico durante un breve período de tiempo

weathering
desgaste climático proceso mediante el cual el viento, la lluvia o el hielo van cambiando y deshaciendo las rocas

Spanish Support

Respuestas

Capítulo 1

Sección 1 Lectura dirigida y repaso
1. "¿Dónde están ubicadas las cosas?" y "¿Por qué están allí?"
2. Les ayudan a los geógrafos a organizar la información.
3. la ubicación absoluta y la ubicación relativa
4. la ubicación relativa
5. Les ayuda a entender la relación entre los lugares.
6. la geografía
7. un paralelo, una línea de latitud
8. un meridiano, una línea de longitud
9. el Meridiano de Greenwich
10. la línea ecuatorial
11. el grado

Sección 1 Examen
1. V
2. F; Las líneas de latitud rodean la Tierra en forma paralela a la línea ecuatorial.
3. V
4. V
5. F; Las líneas de latitud dividen al globo terráqueo en unidades llamadas grados.
6. c
7. b
8. d
9. b
10. a

Sección 2 Lectura dirigida y repaso
1. Los mapas solamente mostraban las zonas por las que la gente viajaba. A veces, algunos lugares no se aparecían en los mapas.
2. Los que hacían los mapas a veces llenaban los espacios en blanco con ilustraciones de tierras míticas y criaturas de leyendas.
3. Los mapas planos son mas fáciles de transportar que los globos terráqueos.
4. Un mapa plano puede mostrar muchos detalles de las comunidades, las ciudades y los estados. Un globo terráqueo tendría que ser muy grande para poder mostrar la misma información detallada.
5. la distorción
6. signos convencionales
7. el globo, a escala
8. la proyección
9. una rosa, los puntos cardinales

Sección 2 Examen
1. d
2. e
3. b
4. c
5. a
6. c
7. d
8. a
9. c
10. a

Actividad de vocabulario
Las oraciones pueden variar. Damos ejemplos de respuestas.
1. El punto cardinal norte aparece en la mayoría de los mapas.
2. La mayoría de los mapas incluye una rosa de los vientos que indica los puntos cardinales.
3. Hay 15 grados entre cada línea de longitud en el mapa del mundo del salón de clases.
4. La proyección de Mercator tiene una distorsión que hace que Groenlandia parezca más grande que América del Sur.
5. La distancia entre la línea ecuatorial y el Polo Norte y el Polo Sur es la misma.
6. Los cinco temas principales de la goegrafía son: la ubicación, el lugar, la interacción de los seres humanos con el medio ambiente, los desplazamientos y las regiones del planeta.
7. Por su forma redonda, un globo es la mejor manera de representar las formas y los tamaños de los continentes y océanos de la Tierra.
8. Cuando no entiendes un símbolo en un mapa, búscalo en los signos convencionales, o inscripciones.
9. El Trópico de Cancer es una línea de latitud que rodea el globo terráqueno a 23.45 grados al norte de la línea ecuatorial.
10. Las líneas de longitud ayudan a los navegantes a averiguar a qué distancia están al este o al oeste de cierto punto.
11. "El Meridiano" es otra manera de decir "la línea de longitud".
12. La razón por la cual las líneas de latitud también se llaman *paralelos* es porque son paralelas las unas a las otras y nunca se cruzan.
13. Algunos mapas indican si una zona es una llanura, una montaña u otra formación geográfica.
14. Los geógrafos miden ubicaciones al este o al oeste del Meridiano de Greenwich.

58 ■ **Recursos del Capítulo y la Sección**   Capítulo 1

Respuestas

15. Los navegantes maritimos han usado la proyección de Mercator por cientos de años.
16. En nuestro salón de clases, hay un mapa de California con una escala de 1 pulgada = 100 millas.

Capítulo 2

Sección 1   Lectura dirigida
1. porque las luces de sus muchas estrellas parecen un vaso de leche derramado por el firmamento
2. porque el eje de la Tierra está inclinado
3. el 20 ó 21 de junio
4. porque las zonas tropicales reciben luz directa del sol
5. el eje
6. altas
7. medias
8. la órbita
9. rotación
10. revolución
11. bajas

Sección 1   Examen
1. e
2. d
3. a
4. c
5. b
6. b
7. c
8. c
9. d
10. a

Sección 2   Lectura dirigida
1. Al observar los continentes hoy en día, parece como si se pudieran poner juntos como las piezas de un rompecabezas.
2. En la década de los sesenta, algunos científicos hallaron fósiles que soportan la teoría de Pangea.
3. La placa de Florida se está moviendo hacia el oeste, de tal manera que cada año la distancia entre Florida y Europa se aumenta en una pulgada.
4. Cuando una placa roza con otra placa se aumenta la presión y se forman volcanes.
5. una montaña, un cerro
6. una llanura
7. una meseta
8. un accidente geográfico
9. una placa
10. las placas tectónicas

Sección 2   Examen
1. V

2. F; Según la teoría de las placas tectónicas, la corteza terrestre está dividida en grandes secciones llamadas placas.
3. F; La partidura de rocas por el viento, la lluvia y el hielo se conoce como desgaste climático.
4. V
5. V
6. c
7. b
8. a
9. c
10. d

Sección 3   Lectura dirigida
1. tiempo
2. corrientes marinas
3. fresco
4. tormentas
5. huracanes, tifones
6. viento
7. los cambios que se dan día a día en el aire, medidos en términos de temperatura y precipitación
8. qué tan frío o caliente es el aire
9. la lluvia, el aguanieve, el granizo o la nieve que cae sobre la tierra
10. el promedio del estado del tiempo durante muchos años

Sección 3   Examen
1. d
2. a
3. e
4. b
5. c
6. c
7. b
8. c
9. a
10. a

Sección 4   Lectura dirigida
1. latitudes bajas
2. latitudes medias
3. latitudes altas
4. bosques húmedos
5. árboles deciduos, flores silvestres, pastos
6. tundra (no hay árboles; sólo arbustos bajos y pastos)
7. tropical y húmedo: dos estaciones húmedas; tropical y seco: una estación húmeda y una seca
8. Hay variación en las estaciones, pero las temperaturas rara vez bajan de cero.
9. veranos cortos y fríos e inviernos largos y fríos

Respuestas

10. las plantas que crecen naturalmente en una región
11. la capa de ramas más alta en la copa de los árboles de un bosque
12. zona fría en la que crecen arbustos y otras plantas bajas, pero no árboles
13. clima que cambia en relación con la altura de una montaña

Sección 4   Examen

1. e
2. a
3. d
4. b
5. c
6. c
7. b
8. b
9. d
10. a

Actividad de vocabulario

1. l
2. m
3. d
4. g
5. o
6. e
7. j
8. c
9. i
10. k
11. f
12. a
13. h
14. b
15. n
16. p

Capítulo 3
Sección 1   Lectura dirigida

1. Los demógrafos investigan los índices de natalidad, de matrimonios y de mortalidad.
2. el 75%
3. las zonas desérticas calurosas, las tierras secas con poca vegetación y las altas montañas
4. en lugares en los que había acceso a extensiones de agua, como ríos o lagos
5. Había tan pocos árboles en la Gran Llanura que los pobladores no tenían recursos para construir viviendas.
6. A través de varias generaciones, la gente que vivía en esos climas aprendió a adaptarse a su medio ambiente.
7. el número total de personas
8. la forma en la que se esparce la población por la Tierra
9. persona que estudia las poblaciones del mundo
10. el número promedio de personas que vive en una milla o en un kilómetro cuadrado

Sección 1   Examen

1. F; Un demógrafo estudia las poblaciones del mundo.
2. V
3. F; La densidad de población es el promedio de personas que vive en una región en particular.
4. V
5. F; El valle del Río Nilo tiene una de las densidades más altas del mundo.
6. b
7. c
8. c
9. a
10. d

Sección 2   Lectura dirigida

1. Los hombres y las mujeres solían vivir menos de 50 años.
2. La población en la mayoría de los países ha crecido rápidamente.
3. Más bebés nacen sanos y la gente vive más años que en el pasado.
4. Las poblaciones en crecimiento consumen los recursos naturales más rápidamente que las poblaciones estables.
5. La gente corta los árboles para usar la madera en la construcción y como combustible.
6. el promedio de vida
7. la revolución verde
8. el índice de natalidad
9. mortalidad

Sección 2   Examen

1. b
2. a
3. c
4. e
5. d
6. b
7. c
8. a
9. d
10. c

Sección 3   Lectura dirigida

1. Durante la revolución cubana de 1958, muchos cubanos fueron "empujados" a los Estados Unidos, en busca de seguridad y una vida mejor.
2. Muchos escandinavos dejaron sus países porque hubo escasez de tierras. Fueron "atraídos" a Minnesota y Wisconsin, donde la tierra era gratis y el clima era similar al de su tierra natal.

Respuestas

3. Muchos habitantes de los Estados Unidos se han mudado a estados del sur y del suroeste del país, en busca de un mejor clima y mejores trabajos.
4. Sao Paulo es el nuevo hogar de muchos brasileños de zonas rurales que han ido allí en busca de mejores viviendas, mejores trabajos y una mejor educación para sus familias.
5. la teoría de "empuje y atracción"
6. emigra, un emigrante
7. urbana, rural
8. urbanización

Sección 3   Examen
1. e
2. d
3. a
4. c
5. b
6. b
7. b
8. a
9. c
10. a

Actividad de vocabulario
Las oraciones pueden variar. Damos ejemplos de respuestas.
1. La población de Chicago, Illinois, es mayor que la de Reno, Nevada.
2. Laura quería averiguar la distribución de la población de Maine.
3. El demógrafo se dio cuenta de que el índice de natalidad iba aumentando más rápido que el índice de mortalidad en la mayoría del mundo.
4. La densidad de población en el desierto de Mojave es bastante baja.
5. El descubrimiento de medicinas modernas es una de las razones por las que el índice de natalidad ha aumentado.
6. El índice de mortalidad es más bajo ahora que hace 200 años.
7. Durante el siglo XIX, el promedio de vida de los hombres y las mujeres en los Estados Unidos era de unos 50 años.
8. Los cambios en la agricultura, como el uso de menos agua en los cultivos y de nuevos fertilizantes para enriquecer la tierra, se conocen como la revolución verde.
9. Durante la fiebre del oro de California hubo una inmigración de gente de la China a los Estados Unidos.
10. Inmigrantes de todo el mundo han llegado a los Estados Unidos.

11. La migración de familias del Sur de Vietnam apoya la teoría de "empuje y atracción", porque las familias fueron "empujadas" a dejar su país a causa de sus enemigos y "atraídas" por la esperanza de una vida mejor.
12. Muchas ciudades están creciendo rápidamente a causa de la urbanización.
13. En las afueras de la ciudad había una zona rural de granjas y pueblos pequeños.
14. Jakarta, Indonesia, es una zona urbana de crecimiento rápido.

Capítulo 4
Sección 1   Lectura dirigida
1. avanzada
2. terrazas
3. la caza y la recolección
4. frías
5. escritura
6. la forma de vida de un grupo de personas que comparten costumbres y creencias similares
7. las destrezas particulares, las costumbres y las maneras de hacer las cosas de un grupo determinado
8. las herramientas y las destrezas necesarias para usarlas
9. los cambios al medio ambiente de un grupo de personas
10. el cultivo de la Tierra y la ganadería

Sección 1   Examen
1. F; La cultura es la forma de vida de un grupo de personas que comparten costumbres y creencias similares.
2. V
3. F; Las destrezas particulares, las costumbres y las maneras de hacer las cosas de un grupo determinado se conocen como rasgos culturales.
4. V
5. V
6. a
7. b
8. c
9. c
10. d

Sección 2   Lectura dirigida
1. En algunas culturas, hay grupos pequeños que trabajan juntos para conseguir comida o proteger la comunidad.

Respuestas

2. Grupos pequeños transmiten las tradiciones y las costumbres de la comunidad y de cada familia en particular.

3. Sin el idioma, los habitantes no podrían transmitir su conocimiento o creencias a las futuras generaciones.

4. El idioma refleja lo que es importante en cada cultura, como por ejemplo las muchas maneras de decir "nieve" en el idioma de los Inuit.

5. una manera de organizar la gente en grupos pequeños

6. la unidad familiar básica en algunas culturas: la madre, el padre y los hijos

7. unidad familiar que incluye miembros de varias generaciones, como los tíos, los abuelos y los primos

8. los estándares de conducta moral de un individuo

Sección 2   Examen

1. d	6. c
2. e	7. b
3. b	8. d
4. c	9. b
5. a	10. a

Sección 3   Lectura dirigida

1. Los individuos y las empresas privadas son dueños de la mayoría de las empresas e industrias de productos básicos y no básicos.

2. El gobierno es dueño de la mayoría de las industrias de productos básicos. Las industrias de productos no básicos pertenecen a individuos o empresas privadas.

3. El gobierno es dueño de todas las industrias. Hay algunas empresas privadas, como por ejemplo, granjas pequeñas o tiendas especializadas.

4. los dueños de las compañías

5. el gobierno

6. el gobierno

7. una monarquía

8. un gobierno

9. un consumidor

10. una democracia directa

11. el capitalismo, el socialismo y el comunismo

12. un dictador

13. una democracia representativa

Sección 3   Examen

1. b	6. b
2. c	7. c
3. a	8. c
4. e	9. b
5. d	10. c

Sección 4   Lectura dirigida

1. las nuevas ideas, la tecnología (como la radio y la televisión)

2. Los "jeans" fueron inventados en los Estados Unidos, pero ahora son populares en todo el mundo.

3. Los japoneses juegan al béisbol, pero han adaptado el juego a su propia cultura.

4. Hoy en día, no es necesario esperar que alguien traiga ideas nuevas de afuera. Ahora las ideas llegan a todo el mundo por fax, teléfono y televisión.

5. porque el transporte y la comunicación moderna pueden conectar casi instantáneamente a personas, empresas y gobiernos lejanos

6. La mayoría de las culturas reciclan y se esfuerzan para proteger los bosques y las especies en peligro.

7. la transmisión de costumbres e ideas de una cultura a otra

8. el proceso de aceptar, tomar prestadas e intercambiar ideas entre culturas

Sección 4   Examen

1. F; La transmisión de costumbres de una cultura a otra se llama difusión cultural.

2. F; La aculturación es el proceso de tomar prestadas ideas entre las culturas.

3. V

4. V

5. F; Si una cultura cambia muy rápidamente, sus habitantes se pueden confudir y la cultura puede llegar a peligrar.

6. b

7. c

8. a

9. d

10. b

Respuestas

Actividad de vocabulario

1.	i	9.	k
2.	m	10.	g
3.	e	11.	j
4.	o	12.	f
5.	b	13.	d
6.	l	14.	h
7.	p	15.	c
8.	n		

Capítulo 5

Sección 1 Lectura dirigida

1. renovable
2. papel, madera
3. renovable
4. alimento
5. reciclable
6. beber agua, bebidas ligeras
7. no renovable
8. para darle energía a los automóviles; para proveer calor
9. cualquier material útil del medio ambiente (como la tierra, el agua, los minerales y la vegetación)
10. un recurso que debe ser cambiado antes de ser usado
11. un recurso natural que tiene un ciclo natural en el medio ambiente (como el agua, el nitrógeno o el carbón)
12. un recurso que puede ser reemplazado (como los cultivos, los árboles y los animales criados para ser usados como alimento)
13. un recurso que no puede ser reemplazado cuando se agote (como el petróleo, el carbón o el gas natural)
14. un recurso no renovable que fue creado hace millones de años por los restos de plantas y animales prehistóricos (como el gas natural o el carbón)

Sección 1 Examen

1.	a	6.	c
2.	d	7.	b
3.	c	8.	c
4.	e	9.	d
5.	b	10.	b

Seccion 2 Lectura dirigida

1. en el segundo nivel
2. la invención de máquinas, la construcción de fábricas y el descubrimiento de nuevas fuentes de energía para crear productos
3. guerras y desastres naturales
4. enfermedades, escasez de alimentos, agua contaminada, educación y servicios de salud deficientes, y gobiernos inestables
5. agricultura comercial
6. ayuda extranjera
7. agricultura de subsistencia
8. plantación
9. en vía de desarrollo, desarrollado
10. manufactura

Sección 2 Examen

1.	e	6.	b
2.	d	7.	c
3.	a	8.	b
4.	b	9.	a
5.	c	10.	d

Sección 3 Lectura dirigida

1. Cuando los bosques húmedos desaparezcan, muchas especies de plantas y animales se extinguirán o morirán.
2. A través de la historia, los seres humanos hemos arrojado productos desechables a los ríos, lagos y mares; esos desechos pueden ser nocivos y pueden destruir las plantas y animales que viven en ellos.
3. Hoy en día, Canadá y los Estados Unidos tienen leyes diseñadas para reducir la polución y así reducir la lluvia ácida.
4. Muchos países han acordado eliminar las sustanciass químicas que destruyen la capa de ozono para el año 2000. Y los científicos están en busca de sustancias químicas que no sean nocivas, para reemplazar los CFCs (clorofluorocarbonos).
5. hábitat
6. la capa de ozono
7. reciclar
8. lluvia ácida
9. calentamiento del planeta

Sección 3 Examen

1. F; Una comunidad de seres vivientes y su medio ambiente se llama un ecosistema.
2. V
3. F; Reciclar es volver a usar materiales para crear nuevos productos.

Respuestas

4. F; El proceso de arrasar los árboles para despejar el terreno se llama deforestación.
5. V
6. b
7. c
8. a
9. d
10. b

Actividad de vocabulario

Las oraciones pueden variar. Damos ejemplos de respuestas.

1. El agua es un recurso natural importante.
2. Los árboles son la materia prima de muchos productos, incluyendo la madera y el papel.
3. El nitrógeno es un ejemplo de un recurso reciclable.
4. Los recursos renovables incluyen las plantas y otros seres vivientes del planeta.
5. El petróleo es un ejemplo de un recurso no renovable.
6. El petróleo es un combustible fósil que se usa en los autos y los camiones.
7. Con la manufactura se crean muchos productos, incluyendo muebles, instrumentos musicales, computadoras y bicicletas.
8. Italia es considerado un país desarrollado, porque tiene muchas industrias.
9. Muchos habitantes de los países en vía de desarrollo viven en zonas rurales.
10. Muchas granjas pequeñas de familia han sido reemplazadas por la agricultura industrial.
11. Mucha gente en los países en vía de desarrollo dependen de la agricultura para su subsistencia.
12. Los trabajadores en las plantaciones, por lo general, cultivan un solo tipo de cosecha (como por ejemplo: la caña de azúcar, el café, el algodón o el plátano).
13. Los países desarrollados a menudo dan ayuda extranjera a los países en vía de desarrollo.
14. Las plantas y los animales sobreviven mejor en sus ecosistemas naturales.
15. Muchos de los bosques húmedos en América del Sur están desapareciendo a causa de la deforestación.
16. Los bosques antiguos de secoyas en la costa oeste de los Estados Unidos son el hábitat de muchas especies de plantas y animales.
17. No hay vida en muchos lagos del norte del estado de Nueva York a causa de la lluvia ácida.
18. Hay evidencia de que la capa de ozono se está volviendo más y más delgada sobre las regiones al sur del planeta.
19. El calentamiento del planeta también se conoce como el efecto invernadero.
20. Hoy en día, es muy importante que reciclemos tanto de lo que usemos que podamos.

© Prentice-Hall, Inc.